C000050485

"Have you ever wondered how the boardroom affects th
no more, the answers are all right here in Jane Gunn's H
and Boredom in the Bedroom!"

— Marshall Goldsmith, million selling author of Wh;
Succession: Are You Ready? and the upcoming *MOJO*

"With this book Jane Gunn provides a breakthrough work much needed when we are bombarded with quick fixes. Jane provides a map to the most important personal development issue there is to achieve success in all aspects of life – interpersonal relationships. This book requires great honesty in your evaluation of yourself and how well you have fulfilled your potential but Jane's refreshing tone with practical illustrations makes that evaluation do-able. Simply put Jane helps us see things in a different way, to see problems differently to overcome obstacles that are often of our own making – follow the guidance in this book and you will arrive at a far healthier place. Brilliant!"

— Colin Ude-Lewis, Author of **Wisdom Notes**

"Jane Gunn's clearly written book has important insights for everyone, not only professionals working in the conflict resolution field. Combining her experience, wisdom, and engaging writing style, she makes a needed and valuable contribution to how conflicts and disputes can be understood and dealt with successfully."

— Dr. Dudley Weeks, International Peacemaker, Author and Speaker

"This is a very enjoyable read, a great book that sucks you in to self analysis – well crafted and full of insight and practical help... I felt like I'd been through therapy..."

— Ian Jones, Head of Publishing and Content, The National Computing Centre

"Most of us think we live in a linear, rational world. This excellent book shows why things are different. It makes the connections that unlock the secrets of reaching and sustaining agreement. It helps the reader to keep their eyes focused on what cannot be seen!"

— Ian Muir, Global Human Resources Director, ESAB Holdings Limited and author of **The Book of Inner Strength – Quotations for Towering Resilience**

"In this work, Jane Gunn, a highly regarded specialist and leading expert in her field, draws on the insights gained from many years of resolving conflict to provide lay audiences with means of detecting conflict and resolving it successfully. The book does not take a timid approach in suggesting that conflict should be avoided. It instead acknowledges it as a necessary part of life, an every day occurrence. Critically, Jane notes that conflict in one area of life can have unintended and often over-looked consequences in other parts of life. And, drawing on her experience, she explains in highly accessible reading, how people can go about connecting symptoms to the problems, and identifying the best solutions for them."

— Michael Mcilwrath, Senior Counsel, GE Oil & Gas, co-author of **International Arbitration & Mediation: A Practical Guide** and host of CPR's biweekly podcast, **International Dispute Negotiation**

"I agree that this is not a sex manual but it is a manual full of stories that help the layman like me to understand and deal with conflict and it also clearly sets out how conflict at home affects work and conflict at work affects home."

— Brian Chernett, Founder, Academy For Chief Executives

"This book has the potential to save you both MONEY and HEARTACHE. Whether you are a CEO, Director, Manager, Business Owner or Employee, if you value your work and your family this book is for you. In it Jane Gunn provides valuable insight and wisdom into how to identify and manage unhappiness and conflict at an early stage before it escalates and becomes both damaging and costly. A VALUABLE read in all senses of the word."

— Dr Tom Hill, Co-Author of *Chicken Soup for the Entrepreneur's Soul*

"This book's great contribution is to render the obvious very readable (with nutshell summaries to help us remember). The world seems slowly to be awakening to the reality that conflict has been too costly for too long and that life on this planet need not be a zero-sum existence. Jane Gunn shows us how we can re-make our world, one relationship at a time. No book could be more highly recommended for the purpose. This one deserves to be read and re-read and to be shared generously with others for the gift it is."

— Jack Levin, Partner & Senior Litigator, Covington & Burling, New York

"Jane Gunn has written an eye-opening, enlightening and empowering book for busy professionals. Act on her advice and it may improve your life forever. Jane is a skilled mediator, successful mother and homebuilder. Her mastery of conflict resolution comes over in a way that is fun to read and easy to digest. It is the kind of book that you can dip repeatedly into and learn more each time. Understand how to improve communication, see beyond "positions" and actually listen properly. What are your family, friends and adversaries really feeling, but not saying? Find out how to figure out what you and they really want. Develop techniques to define what really matters. Heartily recommended!"

— Dr Harjinder S. Obhi , Google's Senior Litigation Counsel EMEA

"I really enjoyed your intuitive and practical guide to achieving more fruitful relationships, thus harmony in all aspects of my life. A must read for anyone looking for a little more peace and happiness!"

— Glenn Watkins, Chief Executive, Ecademy

"This is a wonderful book! It is a great work, invaluable to everybody irrespective of what they do. I cannot even tell where it is more applicable to: the home or the work place. It is in recognition of this fact that you structured each chapter to simultaneously serve both as reflected in the title: How to Beat Bedlam in the Boardroom and Boredom in the Bedroom. Any morning my boss enters the office with a whistle, I know work will be sweet that day and that's thank to his wife (my behind-the-scene or indirect boss). The workplace is actually the place we go to practice what we learn/have learnt at home. (But, please do not change the title. It is a wonderful rhyme)."

— Chris Ameshi, Onshore Project Division, Nigerian Agip Oil Company

HOW TO BEAT BEDLAM IN THE BOARDROOM AND BOREDOM IN THE BEDROOM

BY JANE GUNN

A LIFE CHANGING GUIDE TO HAPPINESS
AT WORK AND AT HOME

Text © Jane Gunn

Cover, book design and layout by Ayd Instone, www.sunmakers.co.uk
Illustrations by Simon Ellinas, www.cartoono.com
Author photography by Haddon Davies
Printed in the UK by TJ International, Padstow

Published in 2010 by HotHive Books, Evesham, UK
www.thehothive.com

The right of Jane Gunn to be identified as the author of this work has been asserted by her
in accordance with the Copyright, Designs and Patents Act 1988.

ISBN: 978-1-906316-47-1

*All characters and stories in this book are fictional, although some may be based on
true events.*

www.corpeace.com

To Sarah
With best Wishes

Jane
November 2016.

To Peacemakers everywhere

"Blessed are the Peacemakers"

Matthew 5.9

ACKNOWLEDGEMENTS

There are so many members of my wonderfully supportive network of family, friends, colleagues, clients and mentors that in their own quiet way have been an inspiration to me and played an important part in the coming together of this book. Thank you all whether you are conscious of your contribution or not.

Very special thanks to:

David Richbell – my friend, colleague and mentor for introducing me to the art of mediation and providing me with the opportunity to grow and develop my skills in this fascinating field of work.

Tom Hill – who inspired me to venture into the world of publishing by declaring "Jane is going to write a book" and never wavering in that belief.

Sue Richardson and Karen Swinden – at The HotHive for their genuine excitement and enthusiasm for this book.

Mindy Gibbins-Klein – "The Book Midwife" who encouraged me to turn ideas into words and chapters.

Lesley Morrisey – a wonderful friend who has edited every word and encouraged every step.

Ayd Instone – for his creative input and design in putting the finished product together with flare and imagination.

Simon Ellinas – for his great sense of fun in creating some wonderful cartoons.

Kriss Akabusi and Steve Head – my A Team for keeping me focused on the task ahead.

My Family – last but not least my husband Rob and daughters Victoria and Rebecca, my greatest inspiration and support.

> *There is no such thing as a "self-made" man. We are made up of thousands of others. Everyone who has ever done a kind deed for us, or spoken one word of encouragement to us, has entered into the make-up of our character and of our thoughts, as well as our success.*
> — **George Burton Adams**

CONTENTS

FOREWORD

by Ambassador Ahmad Kamal
Senior Fellow, United Nations Institute for Training and Research

It is tempting to be carried away by the title of this book, or to misjudge the easy flow of its text. The book can be read in a single sitting, but once that is done, it begins to sink in slowly, and the depth of the connections which it makes between the market-place and the home begin to emerge.

In essence, the lessons that it highlights are fairly simple to assimilate, though most of us either ignore or forget them all the time.

Precepts about tolerance and empathy and compromise are all part of the slogans of public discourse. And yet, when it comes to actual negotiations, we all tend to harden our positions, frequently beyond repair, not realising that win-win solutions are far more durable, and satisfying, than results that just end in winners and losers.

That is what makes this book so enjoyably topical. It is to be hoped that this enjoyment will open the door to success in the boardroom and the bedroom equally.

INTRODUCTION

> "If a woman is unhappy in her relationships, she can't concentrate on her work. If a man is unhappy at work, he can't focus on his relationships."
> — Alan and Barbara Pease

This is not a sex manual!

Before you get excited that this book is a new sex manual designed to enhance your skills in the bedroom, let me explain.

In my work as a mediator I have specialised in the resolution of boardroom, partnership and workplace disputes. I have also coached and run workshops for chief executives and business owners. There are many common themes among the issues that cause unrest and unhappiness between people who work together, but the key thing that strikes me, on nearly every occasion, is the impact of work on home life.

Almost every instance of conflict or dispute at work is the catalyst for, or is mirrored by, conflict at home. In the same way relationships at home have a dramatic impact on our ability to create a productive and harmonious work life.

This experience was highlighted during a workshop I ran recently on how to manage conflict at work for Chief Executives. When we got to the break I joined a group of participants for coffee. It turned out that one of the major problems affecting this group of senior business leaders was how to manage their teenagers at home and how getting this right would transform their lives both at home and at work. As a result we spent the second half of the workshop focused on this issue with each of them taking it in turns to role-play truculent teenagers!

This book seeks to highlight that the same skills and tools can be used to manage conflicts and disputes between individuals, groups of people, organisations and even between nations.

The adversarial approach

Before becoming a mediator, I worked as a corporate lawyer in London. While trying to sell my house to another lawyer I realised that we have created an adversarial culture. I began to wonder whether there might be a better way to help my business clients to manage their affairs.

In the early 1990s Professor Charles Handy challenged a group of business leaders to help him discover the critical factors that would identify 'Tomorrow's Company'.

An enquiry called Tomorrow's Company followed and one of the key findings was that the adversarial approach to relationships is one of the key behaviours that prevents companies from performing at their optimum level.

For me the journey from lawyer to mediator has taken me from adversary to collaborator. Recognising the value of putting relationships first and finding ways to understand what drives and motivates people in dispute.

"The argument culture urges us to approach the world – and the people in it – in an adversarial frame of mind. It rests on the assumption that opposition is the best way to get anything done: The best way to discuss an idea is to set up a debate; the best way to cover news is to find spokespeople who express the most extreme, polarized views and present them as 'both sides'; the best way to settle disputes is litigation that pits one party against the other; the best way to begin an essay is to attack someone; and the best way to show you're really thinking is to criticize... Conflict and opposition are as necessary as cooperation and agreement, but the scale is off balance, with conflict and opposition over-weighted."

— Deborah Tannen

The best outcome

One question that people in dispute frequently find difficult to answer is 'What outcome do you want?'

The basic question 'What are you really looking for?' can lead people to discover surprising things about what is behind their dispute and give them clues as to where the solution may lie.

What doesn't work, at least in isolation, is money. The outcomes that people generally find most satisfying are relational rather than financial.

As psychologist, Martin Seligman, has discovered, human beings flourish whether at work or at home when they have close relationships with other people. You will discover in the pages that follow that most arguments, even when the issue appears to be about money, are, in fact, about love, respect, understanding and the basic human need to know that you matter and are being heard.

> "If I were to summarize in one sentence the single most important principle I have learned in the field of interpersonal relations, it would be this: Seek first to understand, then to be understood. This principle is the key to effective interpersonal communication."
> — Stephen Covey

Everyone is different

I recognise that each of you will have your own style and method of assimilating information. In this book the chapters can be read individually and key messages are often repeated.

If, like me, you like to read a book backwards or appreciate a summary of what you have just read, the last chapter will provide you with just that.

What is true for one person can be entirely different from what is true for another – and that is exactly what this book is about!

What is important is that you are a seeker with an open mind.

> "...what may appear as the truth to one person will often appear as untruth to another person. But that need not worry the seeker. Where there is honest effort, it will be realised that what appeared to be different truths are like the countless and apparently different leaves of the same tree."
>
> — Gandhi

1: BEDLAM OR BOREDOM

How conflict affects us all

> "The quality of our lives depends not on whether or not we have conflicts, but on how we respond to them."
>
> — Tom Crum

BEDLAM

IN THE BOARDROOM

Jim is one of eight directors of a company that manufactures and sells smoothies and juices. Recently, the members of the Board have fallen out about the development and branding of a new product that contains a special blend of herbs and is reputed to have aphrodisiac qualities that the marketing director wants to call 'Blue Heaven'.

Jim thinks they are venturing too far from the company's original vision. Instead of discussing Jim's concerns, his fellow directors have frozen him out of discussions and are making it very difficult for him to carry on with his role as head of the sales team.

Jim has instructed his lawyers to issue legal proceedings. He believes that his fellow directors have deliberately made it impossible for him to do his job well and are now claiming that he is not performing well enough. Jim is feeling hurt and angry, he will not go quietly!

BEDROOM

BOREDOM IN THE

Meanwhile, at home Jim's wife, Sally, is thinking of leaving. Jim seems totally obsessed with his work these days and unwinds by spending even more hours on the golf course.

He has put all his energy into the company over the past few years and seems to have little time left for her!

Things seem to have got even worse over the last few weeks and Jim has retreated even further into his shell refusing to say what is wrong. Sometimes Sally feels as though she is totally invisible and worthless.

Stuff happens

- Your business partner is not pulling her weight

- Your co-director is not a good team leader

- Your employees are demanding a pay rise

- Your husband is late home

- Your neighbours are noisy

- Your teenager won't tidy his bedroom

- Your doctor has misdiagnosed a medical condition.

No matter how hard you try to have a perfect life it just doesn't work that way: stuff happens. Along the way you will experience unhappiness, disappointment, dissatisfaction and unmet expectations – conflict!

I would be surprised if anyone reading this book has not experienced a conflict during the last week. Something or someone has caused you to feel unhappy. It might be something they said (or didn't say) or something they did (or didn't do), or it could be their reaction to something you said or did, but the end result was that you felt unhappy. You felt that the relationship or the situation was not as good as it could be and you didn't know what to do to make things better.

Sometimes our reaction to conflict is to fight. We need to prove that we are right, impose our views or solutions on others even if they fight back. If necessary we will employ others (lawyers and advisers) to help us craft the winning argument and to fight on our behalf.

Sometimes our reaction to conflict is to run away or give in. To give up on the person that we perceive is causing the problem. What's the point in trying any more?

Sometimes when we are tired of being unhappy with a person or situation, we no longer have the energy to fight back.

What if we had the skills and tools to anticipate these unhappy situations before they had a chance to damage our work/life relationships?

What if we understood the *rules* for happy relationships and were able to apply them. How valuable would that be?

The cost

> Jim has already called in his lawyer to help him assess his legal rights and possibly make a claim against the company. His position as Sales Director of a successful company is in jeopardy and, to be honest, he is devoting very little time to developing new sales leads as he has lost all motivation and is spending most of his time managing the situation at work.
>
> Relationships with his fellow directors have disintegrated and he is hardly speaking to his wife. Jim is not sleeping well and when he visited his GP, it was suggested that he might be depressed and should consider taking some time off work – the last thing he can do right now!

Unmanaged or badly managed conflict can have an enormous cost to us all as individuals, businesses and society. It is not always possible to quantify the loss in financial terms, but the loss or waste incurred includes:

- Expert advice – the cost of lawyers, accountants, counsellors, therapists

- Time and productivity – the value of your time devoted to the conflict

- Relationships – the value of a lost or damaged relationship

- Health – the cost to your mental and physical wellbeing.

The cost to British business of unresolved conflict runs into billions of pounds every year.

The cost to families cannot be estimated!

The value

What if Jim and his fellow directors had been able to catch their disagreement before it had escalated into a dispute, and made a commitment to find a way to resolve their differences? How might that benefit the company in terms of productivity and sales and what impact might that have on relationships and organisational culture for the future?

What most people who are experiencing conflict tend to forget is that difference is the source of all value. The general rule is that because each of us has something someone else lacks and we each lack something someone else has; we gain by interaction.

Catching conflict before it becomes destructive and seeking creative ways to resolve problems and keep relationships on track is the key to adding value instead of generating waste or loss.

If both sides to any conflict – a marriage breakdown, business dispute or a bloody war – truly listen to each other, they can eventually reach a resolution.

Warning signs

Conflict is nothing more than a process. It is the process whereby we or others express our dissatisfaction with another or others, or with a situation. When our efforts at expressing our dissatisfaction or unhappiness do not produce positive results or we ignore the warning signs altogether; we edge closer and closer to a crisis.

When the Mount St Helens volcano erupted at 8.23 am on Sunday 18th May, 1980 in Portland, Oregon, USA, people were unprepared and shocked at the devastation that followed. However:

- The eruption occurred *two months* after the mountain first started venting

- There had been *many warning signs* that a devastating blast would happen.

Despite these warning signs, 57 men, women and children were killed. Despite predictions of landslides and floods people were sitting in deckchairs on the bridges to get a better view of the volcano – the watery wall of mud and trees that followed wiped out all the bridges!

Al Siebert[1], a Portland resident who happens to be a psychologist who has studied what it takes for individuals and organisations to survive potentially disastrous events suggests that there are many important lessons to be learnt from natural disasters:

> 1. *We will deny danger or potential disruption if it is inconvenient.*
>
> 2. *Disbelief prevails over reality – even when there are warning signs, most people will dismiss a threat if it has never happened before.*
>
> 3. *Even when people know that problems might occur, they seldom make plans for dealing with them until they actually happen!*

The truth is that we only change course when we are motivated to do so. Our partner leaves us; we are fired from our job; our work team becomes mutinous; someone lodges a formal complaint; a writ arrives on our doormat! Managing conflict is about learning to recognise and pay attention to the warning signs and *knowing what to do* when we receive them. We learn our biggest lessons and experience the most valuable opportunities when things get tough. Having a strategy to work with conflict and crisis is one of the most important things we can do.

[1] The Survivor Personality by Al Siebert

Window of opportunity

If we can pay attention to the warning signs and catch conflict at an early stage, before relationships have broken down and while dialogue is still a possibility, we can save enormous costs and build considerable value.

A window of opportunity exists from the moment that we or others begin to feel unhappy about the way someone is behaving or the way in which a situation is unfolding.

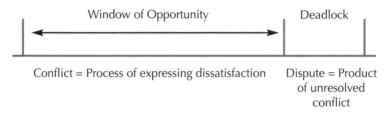

Fig 1.1

Know who and what matters most

How can we apply the principles of conflict resolution to add maximum value and save the most in costs?

Three key principles

1. **Know *who* matters to you and *why*.** Know who is most important to you in your personal and in your business life.

2. **Know *what* matters to them and *why*.** Make sure that you know what matters most to them in terms of your relationship and/or business dealings with them and discover why.

3. **Know *what* matters to you and *why*.** Take time to reflect on what matters most to you and why and learn the best way to communicate this.

If asked, Jim might say that his wife Sally matters most to him in his personal life because she is his constant support and the person that keeps him grounded.

But does Sally *know* that she is the most important person in Jim's life – she certainly doesn't *feel* as though she is.

If asked, Jim might say that *he believes* what matters most to Sally is the house and lifestyle he provides and the social circle they belong to as a result.

But if Jim *asked* Sally what matters most to her, he might be surprised to discover that the house and the lifestyle are pretty low down on her list of priorities. She is more interested in spending her leisure time with Jim and the long-standing friends they made when Jim was less enmeshed in corporate politics and they had a more modest lifestyle. She doesn't have much in common with the smart and superficial acquaintances where they live now.

If Jim took time to ask *himself* what matters most to him, he might find that while he is proud of his achievements at work and of the money and status that follows, it is *relationships* that matter most to him; relationships with his wife, Sally, and with his co-directors; both of which need some attention right now.

Repeating this exercise with his co-directors would provide vital information for Jim to understand how his world and the people and relationships in it fit together.

These are the key principles that underpin every successful relationship, inspired team effort or organisational triumph and explain every disappointment and deadlock.

Changing mindsets

The journey from conflict to resolution requires both foresight and preparation.

The worst times are when things are happening or not happening and we seem powerless to stop them or change them. Then, when it gets worse, we hope that someone outside – an expert or a lawyer – will intervene and put things right.

It reminds me of Kierkegaard's story [1] of the traveller in the hill country who came to a village only to find his road onward blocked by a mountain. So he sat and waited for the mountain to move. Years later, he was still there, old now and white haired, still waiting. Then he died, but he was long remembered as 'the man who waited for the mountain to move'.

But, as you will learn in the chapters that follow, it's not mountains that are the barrier – it's the mindset!

The world is crying out for more people to step out of the prison of their own thinking, to 'break the rules'.

In a nutshell

If we have children or parents or partners or neighbours or colleagues – if we have any relationships at all, we are bound to run into conflict, so we might as well prepare ourselves for it and equip ourselves to cope with it when it happens.

"Somewhere out beyond ideas of right-doing and wrong-doing, there is a field. I'll meet you there."
— Rumi

[1] The Danish philosopher, Søren Kierkegaard (1813–1855)

2: THE MURKY SWAMP OF REALITY

Why people don't say what they think or feel until it's too late

> *"Isn't it strange that we talk least about the things we think most about?"*
>
> — Charles A Lindbergh

BEDLAM
IN THE BOARDROOM

Roger, the chief executive of an IT company, called me one day to ask for my help. 'I have just received another email,' he said. 'It's the third this week and I really don't know what to do next!'

Roger had joined this small family company back in the 1980s and had literally grown with the company, which was now distributing computing products worldwide with subsidiaries in Germany.

What Roger was best at was selling. He just loved the sales side of the business and the rapid growth of the business was mostly due to his sales acumen.

After 18 years in the business Roger was delighted to be offered a seat on the board, it seemed like a great step up from sales manager and a reward for all his hard work so far. Then two years ago, Roger was appointed CEO and now he really did feel as if he had made it.

His family was proud, his colleagues were pleased, but somewhere at the back of Roger's mind was a nagging doubt. Secretly (and Roger didn't dare voice this to anyone) Roger missed his job in sales. He liked all the people he worked with, many of whom had grown up through the company with him, but now he had to manage all the people issues that arose on a day-to-day basis. He was rapidly getting out of his depth.

The current crisis involved the new sales director, Charlie. Roger had interviewed Charlie himself and he seemed a nice enough chap with all the right qualifications. Roger was sure he would settle into the job (that he used to love) given enough time and support.

The other directors did not seem to share his optimistic view. Roger had received a number of 'confidential' emails from some of the other directors complaining about Charlie and suggesting that he wasn't pulling his weight, often coming in late or going early; was not a team player; failed to deliver on promises or actions agreed at meetings; was a poor communicator; failed to lead his team effectively and was generally regarded as the weakest link in the organisation.

Clearly, the other directors were discussing Charlie amongst themselves and then firing emails off to Roger.

On the surface everything was fine. Recent board meetings were conducted without reference to the secret messages passing between the other directors and Charlie was blissfully unaware of the drama unfolding behind the scenes.

BEDROOM

BOREDOM IN THE

Roger feels as though his head is going to explode! All he wants to do is get on with the work of planning a new product launch yet he seems to spend increasing amounts of time dealing with other people's issues.

He is working such long hours now, and most of it doing tasks he doesn't enjoy, that when he eventually gets home at night, all he wants is a stiff drink and to slump in front of the television. At weekends, Roger disappears into his office at home to try and catch up with the never-ending stream of emails he now receives.

Roger's twin daughters, Alice and Millie, often try to distract him from the computer screen. Once they decided to put on a show for him of the dance they would be performing at the school concert that Roger would be unable to attend. Roger tried to focus on the little pink figures twirling in front of his desk, but his mind kept switching back to the latest email on the HR crisis.

Deborah, Roger's second wife, has got tired of expecting him to be home for dinner and most nights she eats with the girls and Roger picks something up on the way home. She would love to tell Roger about her day, how the children's clothing business she has set up is going and what the girls have been up to, but Roger is too tired and distracted and so she doesn't bother.

Most nights at around 10.30 Deborah retires to bed with the latest book she is reading for the book club. Roger feels he must catch up with the latest news and sports results and, more often than not, when he gets to bed Deborah is already asleep.

The thin veneer of sociability

> *"Whatever is unspoken is the hardest to change."*
>
> – Anon

What do the people who matter most to you, in business or at home, really think of you? Do you know how they rate you as a colleague, boss, husband, wife, or lover?

Charlie is blissfully unaware of the situation unfolding at work and how his co-directors feel about him. Roger does not know how to deal with the complaints from his fellow directors and he does not realise the impact that the conflict at work is having on his home life and relationships – no one is talking about the things that really matter.

On what level would you say that you most frequently communicate with those people that matter to you?

- Cliché level – 'small talk' about the weather and other safe topics

- Reporting facts – discussing news items and other facts and information

- Sharing of opinions – ideas and beliefs about life and/or a current situation

- Sharing feelings – I feel anxious, angry, happy

- Total honesty and openness.

Most of the problems we encounter in our day-to-day life whether at home or at work are with other people, and sometimes other people encounter problems with us. Do they tell you? Do you tell them?

How often do you exchange friendly greetings with someone or even work or live alongside them and yet bad mouth them or talk about their shortcomings behind their back?

Why do we find it so difficult to let someone know that we are unhappy and that all is not well?

One of our greatest needs as humans is to socialise and to be sociable and so one of our greatest fears is that we will upset, offend or repel those that we want to socialise with. As a result, we often fail to deal with problems and issues in our relationships until they have blown up and become even more scary and difficult to address.

Do you remember being a child at school and not being sure who would want to be your friend and sometimes arriving at school in the morning to find that your 'friends' were no longer speaking to you and you were all alone?

Children who are just learning to get along with each other often react instinctively to things that other children have said or done. They can be quite direct with their pals as to why they are no longer in favour: 'you smell'; 'you pinched my rubber'; 'you copied my homework' – hurtful, but honest!

As a child these blips in relationships often don't last very long and we find new or even pretend friends to fill the gap. My sister, Clare, had an imaginary friend called 'Loggy Loggy' who, quite conveniently, lived in a house that we passed each day on the way to school. As we walked by

Clare would remind herself that here lived her best friend of all. Whatever happened at school she knew that she would pass by his house again on the way home and feel glad that she still had one true friend.

Adults on the other hand rarely find it straightforward to talk about concerns with each other, because the consequences of a broken relationship are so much more complex. We might hurt a friendship or lose a job if we say the wrong thing.

Our true thoughts and feelings are often hidden behind the *thin veneer of sociability*. Signs and gestures such as a smile or handshake and clichéd conversation can create an illusion of safe and friendly relations and enable us to delay dealing with important issues – sometimes for years.

How well do we really know each other?

Your boss Jeremy is impossible; he is unreasonable and demanding. He expects you to stay late and to cover for him at meetings. He rarely acknowledges your contribution. He creates chaos around him and you find working with him unbearably stressful.

Then Jeremy dies unexpectedly. You go to his funeral and you are surprised that there are hundreds of people attending. Several people speak at the service, they talk about Jeremy as a kind and generous man; they mention his charity work and his devotion to his nieces and nephews; they liken him to a diamond with many different facets.

You think about the diamond and you realise that you didn't really know Jeremy at all. While you didn't manage to raise with Jeremy the issues that were affecting your working relationship and causing you to think of leaving the company, you also didn't find a way to discover the real Jeremy.

The mask or veneer we use to front our communications with others can both prevent them from knowing us well so that they *don't appreciate our good points* and deter them from raising issues that are affecting our relationship so that we are *unable to deal with our bad points*.

Do you have the skills and do you devote the time to building strong relationships with the people that matter most to you? If you can communicate with them on a deeper more meaningful level and be more honest with each other when things are not going well you'll find your relationships will be more rewarding and the results you achieve less stressful in the process.

What do you expect?

> *"Marriage means expectations and expectations mean conflict."*
>
> — Plaxton Blair

You are going to buy a new pair of shoes, attend an important meeting to discuss a new project or go out to dinner with your partner. Whatever the event, you have an *expectation* of how it will be; how people will behave; what they might say; agreements that will be reached and, if things are not as you expected – the shop assistant was inattentive and sold you the wrong size shoes, your boss was dismissive of your work on the project, your partner was late home and you missed the restaurant booking – you are likely to be *unhappy*.

All conflict springs from differing expectations, competing goals, conflicting interests, confusing communications or unsatisfactory relationships. In short, a person did not behave as we wanted them to and we are hurt, confused, angry or simply puzzled.

Why did Roger expect that Charlie would be successful in the role of sales director? What did the other board members expect of him? How did they expect Roger to deal with the situation? What are Deborah's *expectations* of Roger as a husband and father?

Sometimes our expectations are *expressed* – we may discuss or even write down what we expect, for example, if we enter into a contract. But more often our expectations are *implied* – even where a formal contract exists sometimes we do not take the time to confirm the attitudes and behaviour we expect or value.

Usually the real cause of conflict is *unmet* expectations – either we did not take the time or we did not know what we needed to say to make our expectations clear and explicit.

How do you show that you're unhappy?

Mary isn't talking to Fred. He arrived home from work late last night and forgot that it was their anniversary.

Grant is in Colin's office discussing the shortcomings of their boss, Helen. According to them, she is a power hungry bully and is making their lives a misery.

Warren is standing on his neighbour's doorstep with a loaded shotgun. He has reached the end of his tether in their long running argument about the enormous hedge.

Conflict is quite simply the process of people expressing their dissatisfaction with one another. It may take the form of:

- Silence – not speaking to one another

- Talking behind someone's back – gossip and innuendo

- Withholding information

- Sabotage

- Fighting – verbal or physical.

How do you show that you are unhappy with someone or something?

Do you sulk or retreat into your shell and expect them to guess that something is wrong? Do you get angry and shout or slam the door? Do you discuss the situation behind their back or plot and scheme to get your revenge?

People express their dissatisfaction in different ways depending on their own past experience of how to handle disagreements. Their reaction may be *active* shouting, angry words or physical violence, or it may be *passive* bullying, sabotage or gossip.

Actually, conflict can be a very good thing. If we never experienced a sense that things are not OK as they are, there wouldn't be any reason to change.

Dissatisfaction is a *catalyst*. It helps us to become aware when something isn't right and encourages us to search for ways to make it better.

What we need most are the skills and tools to help us to explore and communicate the depths of our dissatisfaction and unmet expectations and to resolve conflict before it becomes dispute. Feeling safe to sometimes *drop the mask* and to *express* our own dissatisfaction at the right time and in the right way can enable us to address issues and to have deeper and more meaningful relationships with others.

- If, instead of sulking in silence, Mary could find a better way to express her unhappiness and dissatisfaction to Fred, perhaps they would be able to celebrate their anniversary instead of continuing the damage to their relationship.

- If Grant and Colin could find a way to alert Helen about how she is perceived by others at work without the fear of reprisals, perhaps they could begin the process of creating a more satisfactory working environment.

- If only Warren felt that it was possible to communicate with his neighbour about the hedge, he would not feel that the only way he could be heard is to threaten him with a shotgun.

As Gerry Spence said in his book *How to Argue and Win Every Time*, "In essence, we remain prehistoric in our approach to conflict. In emotional terms we have not developed as fast as the world around us – this in itself is a conflict. We must learn simple, but effective ways to communicate with one another. How to speak and how to listen. How to communicate honestly to achieve our needs and realise our dreams, rather than splattering human bodies across the landscape whether metaphorically or in reality."

The earlier we can alert our family members, partners, co-workers or neighbours of our unhappiness, the more likely we are to be able to have a constructive dialogue and look for mutual solutions rather than create a destructive spiral of sulking, backbiting, sabotage and even violence. Sometimes, we need the help of someone outside the situation to help facilitate a safe exchange of views.

With the help of a conflict management consultant, Roger and Charlie were able to safely explore and communicate the real issues between them and to create the basis of a more constructive working relationship. Roger was able to discuss, at least privately, the strain that his promotion to CEO was having on his relationships as work and at home and to seek help and support where he most needed it, delegating some of the tasks he found most difficult to other directors.

Now when Roger gets home from work he can focus on his daughters and on Deborah instead of continuing to worry about life at the office.

In a nutshell

Good and bad points in a relationship are hidden behind a mask or veneer of sociability. Creating a safe way to address issues and concerns is the key to constructive resolution and deeper relationships.

"I've always believed that a lot of the troubles in the world would disappear if we were talking to each other instead of about each other."

— Ronald Reagan

3: AN ISLAND IN PARADISE

Why you and I see the same things differently

> "Nothing other people do is because of you. It is because of themselves. All people live in their own dream, in their own mind; they are in a completely different world from the one we live in. When we take something personally, we make the assumption that they know what is in our world, and we try to impose our world on their world."
>
> — Don Miguel Ruiz

BEDLAM

The other day, Faisal came into the office of his business partner, Gill, and told her in no uncertain terms that he was fed up with her behaviour and attitude towards the small accountancy practice of which they are both partners.

Faisal became quite angry during the exchange between them and told Gill that ever since she joined the partnership six years ago, she had not pulled her weight, often missing partners' meetings and that she had failed to bring in many new clients or take an active role in developing the business.

Gill was astonished by Faisal's sudden outburst and his aggressive tone towards her, as he thumped the table and raised his voice.

She tried to explain that having decided to return to work following full maternity leave for the birth of her two children, Sam and Ben (6 and 4), she was now doing her best to combine motherhood and career. She explained that the recent diagnosis of Ben's autism has caused her a lot of stress and the need to rethink childcare arrangements at home.

Faisal replied that he and his wife have always regarded his wife's role as staying at home to look after the children, especially when they are ill and that, in the Middle East where his family comes from, this is what is expected of a good wife.

Gill was outraged, how dare Faisal assume that she didn't value her role as a wife and mother just because she had chosen to return to work. She accused Faisal of bullying her by shouting and being aggressive and that as a practising Buddhist she was committed to non-violence and found his behaviour deeply offensive.

The above story illustrates the beginning of a very typical partnership dispute but how can Gill and Faisal reconcile their very different views and attitudes?

BEDROOM

BOREDOM IN THE

Gill is exhausted by the conflict at work and the stresses and strains of dealing with an autistic child. Julian, her husband, has recently set up his own business as a consultant and is feeling exasperated by Gill's daily rants about Faisal and the partnership. He would much rather be focusing on his own needs and unwinding with a gin and tonic.

Gill feels that Buddhism offers her the calm she cannot seem to find anywhere else and has recently become a vegetarian in the hope that it may help her to feel healthier and also may help with Ben's autism.

Gill cannot understand why Julian does not see things her way. Why does he not share her passion for raw food or embrace her new religion with the same enthusiasm that she does? He seems to be happier spending his time with his mates in the pub. Gill fears that they are growing apart, unable to see why the other refuses to change.

The world as you see it

Why are we so attached to, and protective of, our own version of events and to our own beliefs and values? Why is it so difficult to accept the legitimacy of other people's views and beliefs?

> *Imagine that you live on a beautiful island surrounded by warm, crystal clear waters with white sandy beaches and covered in lush vegetation and stunning plants and flowers. The weather is perfect with gentle sunshine and the occasional showers to refresh and replenish the gardens and a small inland lake provides fresh drinking water. The fruits, vegetables, nuts and seeds growing there, together with the fish in the sea and lake are enough to provide you with all the nourishment you need.*
>
> *Your shelter on the island and the landscaping are all your own creation, built up piece by piece over the years. You know each twist and turn of the pathways, the scent of every blossom and flower, the feel of the sand running through your fingers. You are comfortable with and comforted by everything around you that you have created. This is your island in paradise.*

This is simply the world as you see it

Everything that has happened to us from the moment we are born influences the way we see and experience the world around us and the people we meet.

All our experiences to date have created the knowledge, attitudes, values, beliefs and convictions that form *our individual view of the world*. It is as though each of us is living on our own personal island. We are familiar with our own territory, with each twist and turn of the road, with each mountain and valley, every plant and tree.

Occasionally, the landscape may change a little as we experience something new that changes our attitudes, values or beliefs but we are comfortable with the way the world looks from there. To us it's paradise!

Each and every one of us makes sense of the external world with reference to our own metaphorical island. Our island creates for us our foundation or roots. It forms the basis of our personal identity and gives us a deep sense of security. It defines who we are. We feel at home there. We imagine that everyone must live on an island similar to, if not the same as, our own.

Having established our island, we interpret everything that we see, hear or experience according to *our pre-existing view of the world*, the frame within which we are already operating.

A couple of years ago I paid a visit to the Adidas Wellness Clinic in Manchester. At the clinic, they run a programme for cardiac fitness and rehabilitation. I handed my business card to the security guard to have a pass made up, it said quite clearly – Jane Gunn, Corporate Peacemakers. My security tag listed me as being from Corporate *Pacemakers*. The guard had interpreted the information on my card with reference to the environment he existed in.

Mindsets of all kinds have the same effect. Religious values and beliefs, professional speciality and attitudes related to age, gender or race. Each filters out the possibility that any other mindset might be right.

Let's look again at the situation involving Gill and Faisal. They view the current situation from such fundamentally different standpoints created from their pre-existing attitudes, values and beliefs.

- Gill believes that it is acceptable to work full time while her children are young, but expects some understanding from her business partner when she needs to focus on family issues rather than work or spend time attending to her disabled son.

- Faisal believes that women should not devote themselves to work when their children are young and especially when they are sick or disabled and, therefore, require extra care and attention.

- Faisal does not expect to cut Gill any slack in relation to her partnership responsibilities. Her priority when she is at work should be to focus on the business.

- Gill is shocked at the manner in which Faisal addresses his concerns to her, she feels his behaviour, shouting and banging the desk, is akin to bullying. As a Buddhist, Gill believes that people should be gentle with each other whatever the issue or complaint.

- Faisal is used to expressing his emotions in a demonstrative way. Shouting when he is upset or angry seems perfectly normal to him, and his friends and family would normally join in. It is part of his personality and his culture to be both dominant and expressive.

The problem is that each of them has failed so far to acknowledge or to take into account the other's views and pre-existing mindset.

Why don't we understand each other?

What happens then when someone from a very different island to ours comes along? We automatically interpret everything that they say and do as if they lived on an island exactly like ours.

If it becomes clear to us that they do not share our view of the world, we are at a loss as to how to bridge the gap. Our instinctive reaction is to *defend our views* and to *reassert our opinions* in the belief that we can persuade or, if necessary, force them to change their mind and enable us to remain safe – but, what if they won't?

When we are forced to meet or communicate with someone who has a totally different set of values, attitudes and beliefs to ours, their initial efforts to persuade or, worse still, force us to see things from their point of view are often unsuccessful. This is because we have been given a very basic interpretation of what they believe and why. It is as though they have shown us a badly drawn map of their island – *we do not get the true picture at all!*

The information that is missing is *how* and *why* they see things as they do. What is most important to them about their views and beliefs.

Instinctive reactions

Our instinctive reaction to difference and to conflict is to *defend* our ideas and our beliefs often to the extent of being aggressive or violent.

Gill cannot understand why Faisal does not see the partnership issue from her point of view or why her husband Julian does not share her views on Buddhism and vegetarianism. She tries to emphasise that she is *right*, repeating what she believes as though she is preaching. Why are Faisal and Julian so stubborn and defensive?

When we are in conflict with someone else, what we want most of all is for them to resolve the situation by automatically *understanding our position* and *accepting our point of view*. We find it impossible to imagine that they do not see the reasonableness of our position and see that the obvious solution is to give us what we want. We do not expect them to be distracted by their own attitudes, values and beliefs.

Do they not see the world as we see it? Is their island not like ours? If not, can they not see that our world is perfect and theirs is not! Don't they long to live in a place just like ours?

The stronger we are in our beliefs and values, the more perfect our world seems to us and the more we resist any message that challenges this view. We prefer to surround ourselves with people and communications that reinforce the views we already have and that continue to make us feel safe and comfortable.

When someone challenges our view of the world, we instinctively *feel threatened* and we behave as though we are under attack. Far from persuading us to change our mind their arguments only serve to increase our resolve and reinforce the very view they so wanted to change. Our view of the world forms the very basis of our personal identity and security. When it is attacked our only response is *to defend* and *to reinforce*.

I must learn about your world

What can you do when your communications with another person have reached deadlock because you cannot understand where they are coming from, cannot see what's important to them and why?

What you need to do, and it is one of the most difficult things of all to do, is to stop judging them as wrong and stop trying to force your view on them. Instead you must become *open and genuinely curious*.

You must be prepared to visit my metaphorical island with an open mind, and be prepared to listen, to learn and to understand. You must be willing and able to imagine just what it would be like if you yourself had lived all your life on this island, had seen what I had seen, shared the same experiences, dreamed the same dreams and suffered the same fears.

This is the most important work of relationships in general and especially of conflict resolution. What I most need to learn about, to acknowledge and to show my understanding of is *your perspective* on the situation.

Faisal needs to gather from Gill enough information to *really understand* her situation and then to say something like: 'I can hear from what you have told me that you are having a tough time right now trying to fulfil your work duties and to deal with Ben and I understand that the partnership is important to you as well as your family…'

Now, instead of trying to persuade Gill that he is right, Faisal is *acknowledging* that she has her own values and beliefs. This simple act may enable them to let go of the need to attack and defend and instead to seek information to help each of them to understand what is *most important* to the other.

Faisal may discover that his *assumption* that family is not important to Gill is not correct, but that her husband, Julian, having recently started a new business, cannot earn enough to support the whole family. What is *most important* to Gill is that they have sufficient income so that they do not run the risk of losing their family home.

Gill, on the other hand, instead of trying to *persuade* Julian to change his eating habits and getting locked in another battle, could start by *acknowledging* the legitimacy of his view that relaxing with a drink is OK (even though she prefers to drink beetroot juice) and discover that, because he works from home, what is *most important* to Julian is being able to differentiate between family and work time. Giving him this space may mean that he no longer feels the need to escape to the pub!

If Faisal, Gill and Julian can stop *making assumptions* about each other's behaviour and stop trying to persuade each other that only their way of seeing and doing things is the right one, then they can prevent the negative cycle of attack and defence and start a dialogue that can help them to really understand one another.

If not, they will remain locked in a battle which cannot be won.

So why do we ignore this common sense approach and continue to focus on ourselves?

Paradise lost

What if someone is not so certain of their beliefs and values, does that make them easier to deal with?

People who have not been able to create a strong vision of their island often lack confidence and find it difficult to settle on the core values and beliefs that they need to feel safe and happy. It is as though their island lacks definition, and if you asked them to describe it in detail they would be unable to do so. Such people often appear to us to be vulnerable, confused and indecisive.

On the other hand, people who are rigid and inflexible in their thinking and who see no possibility for change of any kind to the island they have built may be unwilling to think new thoughts or to learn from new experiences. Their island no longer represents paradise, but is more like a prison preventing them from communicating effectively with the world outside.

Sometimes things happen that are *beyond our control* and which threaten our happiness and security. Just as a natural disaster, a flood, earthquake or fire might destroy part of our real habitat, so emotional disasters such as redundancy, divorce, bereavement and illness can damage our world view.

When this happens, we may experience a frightening sense of doubt and loss of clarity of our values and how to deal with the outside world. Then we have to focus all our efforts on rebuilding and repairing our island.

Sometimes we are so desperate to rebuild and repair, to re-establish what we have lost that we adopt a whole new set of values, attitudes and beliefs. Examples of this include:

- Embracing a fanatical religion or extreme political party

- Falling in love on the rebound with someone hopelessly inappropriate

- Turning anything: work, alcohol, food, or another person, into the central focus of our lives.

Any of these can be an attempt to build or recreate a sense of security and safety that is vital to our mental and physical wellbeing.

Having strong views may make us feel confident and able to deal with the world beyond our shores. However, having a perspective that is dynamic rather than static enables us to accommodate other views and beliefs and to accept and adapt to change.

In a nutshell

We interpret everything we see, hear or experience according to
our pre-existing view of the world and our instinctive reaction to
difference and conflict is to defend our ideas and beliefs. Being
prepared to learn about, understand and acknowledge each
other's perspective is the key to good relationships and to
resolving conflict.

"The only paradise is paradise lost."

— Marcel Proust

4: PERFORMANCE ISSUES

How do you behave in response to conflict?

> *"Life has no rehearsals only performances."*
>
> – Anon

BEDLAM

IN THE BOARDROOM

Joe Smith was the founder of a hugely successful soft drinks company. As Chief Executive and owner of 47 per cent of the company, he suddenly found himself subject to a vote of no confidence when sales fell and stock prices tumbled sharply.

With management of the company in turmoil, a number of Joe's fellow directors conspired to remove him as CEO and Joe faced the prospect for the first time of no longer being in overall control of the company and consequent loss of status.

Joe was determined to fight back and teach the young upstarts a lesson. He enlisted two other shareholders to fight with him increasing the voting power to over 50 per cent and called a shareholders' meeting. The vote was carried and Joe succeeded in ousting the five directors who had been plotting against him.

BEDROOM

BOREDOM IN THE

Joe met his wife, Alice, when they were both just out of university and worked in a young and thrusting marketing firm. They loved to chew over the details of their more challenging projects and socialise with other high earning colleagues.

Alice is now the proud mother to Bryony. She works part time and no longer stays late to drink. Her focus and priorities have changed and she wishes that Joe would give up the late night working and drinking.

But Joe has a different baby to worry about: his company; and all his efforts are focused on trying to stay in control. Their paths hardly seem to cross these days. Alice knows that Joe is under pressure and she doesn't want to add to the burdens of the working week. So these days she travels home early and with the baby safely tucked up in bed opens a bottle of chilled Chablis and drinks alone to drown her sorrows.

Automatic responses

The other day I was working in the office at the top of my house. It was late on a winter's afternoon and already dark outside. Without warning the power was cut, my PC shut down and the whole house was plunged into darkness.

We have no street lights in our road and when I raised my hand in front of my face I couldn't even make out the shape of my fingers – it was pitch black. By chance, I had received an email earlier that day from our Neighbourhood Watch representative with a warning from the police about bogus meter readers and my daughter reported letting a meter reader into the house the day before.

I looked out of the window to see whether other houses were also experiencing a power cut, but no, their lights were shining brightly into the gloom. Immediately my imagination went into overdrive. What if this was not a simple power cut! What if someone had deliberately thrown the power switch downstairs!

Now instinct took over. My heart started to beat faster as I thought quickly what to do. I felt my way to the door of my office and started to edge down the stairs. Then I heard a noise. I crept into our bedroom on the floor below my office and located my husband's cricket bat behind the door.

Now armed for combat, I continued towards the ground floor ready to confront an intruder.

But when I reached the bottom of the house there was no sign of any intruder and I realised that my mind had gone into overdrive and caused me to react to an imagined fear.

Amygdala spin

What is it that makes us react so quickly and instinctively when threatened?

There is a primitive part of our brain called the *Amygdala*. The job of this tiny almond-shaped part of the brain is to detect anything that might be a potential threat to our survival. The Amygdala acts fast, much quicker than the logical, thinking part of our brain, and the only answers it provides us with are:

- Fight

- Flee

- Freeze

- Appease.

The Amygdala acts on the *perception of threat*. That is, it does not give us time to check out whether the threat it is real or imagined. Any conflict, that is anything that threatens our needs and interests, or our values, attitudes and beliefs, is reacted to as if it were an immediate threat to our survival.

A social threat is treated in same way as a physical threat.

Imagine that you have a difference of opinion with your partner. Unable to 'persuade' him or her to your point of view you begin trading insults. In the moment that your brain registers an insult, it reacts as if it had met with a lion or an intruder. The Amygdala bypasses the cerebral cortex, which is the logical thinking part of the brain and you react immediately by choosing to fight back, walk away, freeze like a rabbit in the headlights or try to pacify and give in to your partner.

It takes enormous self-restraint and wisdom to pause and to consciously choose an alternative response to a perceived threat. A fast reaction may be good for surviving physical danger, but it's not so good for managing situations of conflict in a calm and measured way.

Whenever something happens that interferes with us getting what we want or creates a situation that is not what we expected our brain may *perceive* it as a threat. We immediately flip into survival mode and *react instinctively* to the threat.

What then happens is that we *defend our perceptions*. The most important thing for the Amygdala is not to lose face and so whatever our initial reaction to a person or situation we stick with it. Changing our minds would create the same feelings of *threat* as the original event.

This is the reason why Joe will justify his decision to fight to be reinstated as CEO and Alice will justify her decision not to challenge Joe about his late nights and drinking.

How do you react?

Think back to the last time that you were in a situation where your instinctive reaction to conflict snapped into play. What did you do?

- Did you fight – use physical or verbal aggression?

- Did you flee – storm off or walk away from the situation?

- Did you freeze – react as though nothing had happened?

- Did you appease – try to stop the conflict by offering concessions?

Each of us has a preferred response to conflict. Some people automatically choose to fight back yet others prefer to run away. We have learnt from past experiences to behave in a particular way and it is very hard to break the pattern of response in the heat of the moment.

You are walking in the jungle and come across a roaring lion if you:

Fight – you will try to kill or maim the lion with physical force or weapons until it is no longer a threat to you.

Are you a fighter?

- Your first instinct is to use whatever power you have – physical, intellectual, status or economic to win and overpower your foe.

- Fighters are primarily concerned with their own needs and interests and not terribly worried about the needs and interests of their opponents.

Flee – you will try and outrun the lion or find a place to hide until the danger has passed.

Are you a fleer?

- Your first instinct is to walk or run away – to put some distance between you and the person or situation causing the conflict.

- Fleers may sensibly be withdrawing from a threatening situation, for example, to avoid physical violence. They may also be sidestepping an issue or postponing dealing with it until later.

- Fleers are not at all comfortable in situations of conflict and are not immediately worried about their needs and interests or those of their opponent. Their motivating force is to avoid the situation altogether – at least for the time being.

Freeze – you will stand or lie completely still in the hope that the lion will ignore you.

Are you a freezer?

- You will not immediately do anything. The hope is that if you do nothing the moment of threat will pass and you can carry on where you left off.

- Rabbits in headlights are rarely safe and real conflict is unlikely to be resolved without some action.

Appease – you will offer the lion some meat or a dead animal to feed on.

Are you an appeaser?

- You would rather give in to the other person's wishes or point of view than make a fuss. You will back off in an argument and tolerate behaviour that you dislike rather than take a stand.

- Appeasers are more concerned in satisfying the needs and interests of the other party in a conflict and not very comfortable articulating their own needs and concerns.

Other factors

What else determines how you may react when you feel under threat?

- Past experience – if something bad has happened to us in the past, our subconscious brain remembers and reacts in the same way when it perceives a similar threat. This is why soldiers suffering from shell shock react to any noise, such as firework exploding, as if they were back in the battle zone. We learn our responses to conflict and threat from what has happened to us before and from our observation of others such as our parents.

- Stress – if we are already under stress whether at work or at home, our brain will be on alert for anything that might tip us over the edge and so we may over-react to perceived threats.

- Food – low blood sugar can affect our brains as can caffeine, alcohol and drugs.

- Sleep – lack of sleep can seriously impair our thinking and make us short-tempered.

Whole brain solution

Instead of reaching for the cricket bat, my instinctive reaction could have been to stay frozen at my desk; to attempt to hide in a wardrobe or under a bed or to head downstairs to 'give in' to the intruder and tell him to take whatever he came for.

It is possible to teach ourselves to have the *whole brain* working in situations of threat or conflict. We have to accept that what we *first experience* is instinctive and not reasoned.

Then we have to ask ourselves three questions:

1. What's really happening here – is this a real emergency?

2. What are some alternative realities to my original perception?

3. Who else matters – what matters to them?

In fact, when I eventually crept downstairs ready to confront the intruder, I discovered that there was nobody there at all! All I needed to do was to feel my way to the electricity meter and flip the switch and the darkness and my fear and suspicion disappeared.

For Joe, his original perception is that his fellow directors want to oust him from his position of leadership and take over the running of the company that he has worked so hard to build. His initial reaction is simply to *fight* back and defend his territory.

Some alternative realities to Joe's original perception might be a genuine concern on the part of his fellow directors about the direction the company is taking. It is also possible that his fellow directors have some real issues with Joe's leadership and decision-making. Trying to uncover these alternative realities and negotiating a solution could be more valuable than a boardroom battle.

For Alice, her original perception is that the company is far more important to Joe than she is or Bryony is. She feels threatened by this, but her instinctive reaction is to *freeze*, and to deal with the issue by drinking alone. As Alice's mother used to drink, *past experience* has an influence on her reaction and behaviour as does the fact that she is *tired and stressed* looking after Bryony on her own.

Some alternative realities to Alice's original perception might be that Joe does not prefer corporate life to family life, but has some genuine issues at work that he has not felt able to discuss with her – perhaps because he doesn't want to worry her. Another alternative may be that, deep down, Alice is frustrated spending all her time at home with Bryony and is reacting to that as much as to Joe's behaviour.

If Alice and Joe were then to consider their relationships, both in the office and at home, they could decide who else matters and what matters to them. It might be possible to override their instinctive reactions, talk about their concerns and look for alternative solutions – before it's too late.

In a nutshell

Our instinctive reaction to conflict is to see it as a threat and to fight, flee, freeze or appease.

Once we understand this we can take time to ask ourselves questions about the situation and use our whole brain to consciously decide what the best response would be.

> *"The trouble with most people is that they think with their hopes or fears or wishes rather than with their minds."*
>
> — **Will Durant**

5: DO POSITIONS MATTER?

Why needs, interests, fears and concerns are more important than the position or stand someone takes on an issue

> *"Nothing is more difficult than the art of manoeuvres for advantageous positions."*
>
> — Sun-Tzu 400 BC

BEDLAM
IN THE BOARDROOM

Phil is distraught, after many years of loyal service to Jen and Terry's, the family-run ice cream business, he no longer has a job.

The recession has hit them hard and sales of their up-market organic ice cream have fallen by 50 per cent. Without any warning, Terry called Phil into his office last week and told him that he was dismissed and should leave that very afternoon. Phil knows that the job market is tough and at the age of 58 he does not stand much chance of finding a similar position.

Despite his friendly relationships with the company's owners, Phil feels incensed at the way he is being treated and the amount of money he is being offered. Rather than talk to Jen and Terry he has gone straight to his lawyers who have advised him on his legal position – they have told him that he is entitled to more money and should issue a claim immediately.

Phil is determined to stand up for his rights and claim every penny he is due. He is meeting regularly with his lawyer to work on his claim and the legal costs are mounting.

This morning Phil met with his brother-in-law, Walter. Walter is running a successful business delivering fresh fish to the restaurant trade. Walter has offered Phil a chance to join the fish business, but what he needs is to find a refrigerated van so that he can help with the fish deliveries.

Phil is searching for a second-hand van but cannot find anything that he can afford. He needs to find £10,000 in ready cash, but he can't afford that sort of money now with his legal fees and living expenses.

BEDROOM

BOREDOM IN THE

Jen and Terry are fighting hard to keep their business afloat and every conversation at home is now about money and banking, stock and cash. Jen and Terry just don't have time for each other as a couple any more. Recently Jen has been dreaming of selling the business and sometimes even thinks of leaving Terry. Family life is suffering and their children Ben and Jo have begun to feel that they don't exist any more. They have also heard whispers that they may have to leave their private schools next term and leave all their friends behind.

Fighting the redundancy claim from Phil is just another headache that Jen and Terry could do without. But at the moment they cannot afford to make the sort of pay-out that Phil wants and so they will instruct their lawyers to fight their position. In the meantime, they have got ice cream unsold and a fleet of refrigerated vans sitting idle!

Why positions are important

Phil's position is that he has been treated badly by his long-standing employers who he regarded as friends, and is determined to fight for what he believes he is entitled to.

Jen and Terry's position is that they are right in the stand that they have taken and for the sake of the business must fight to defend Phil's claim.

When we take a particular stance on an issue – we are *for* foxhunting or *against* war – we say that is our position on the matter.

So in terms of conflicts and disputes, position can be used to establish our power or influence in relation to others and it can put down a marker for our view on the issue.

The main thing about a position is that once we have one and particularly if we perceive it to be to our benefit or advantage we do not want to move, to change or to let it go.

Conventional dispute resolution involves each person taking up a position and then through a process of power struggle, strutting and posturing, bluff and counter-bluff and, often assisted by lawyers and experts, seeking to disprove and discredit the other person's position and show that they were right all along.

Positions signal what a person wants the rest of the world to know.

From the moment that we become aware of ourselves as individuals, positions become important to us. Position is often linked to our identity and therefore important to saving face. We do not want to be perceived as weak by giving way on our position.

But what positions do not tell you is what a person *really* wants to achieve and *why*.

Needs and interests

So what do Phil and Jen and Terry really need as opposed to what they say they want and why?

Just like an iceberg, hidden beneath the surface of each party's publicly declared position is a mass of information about their very personal needs and interests, fears and concerns which in reality matter far more to them than simply proving that they are right.

All people are motivated in disputes to hold on to and enforce their positions by

- Fundamental *needs* – where absence would cause so much pain that they are not negotiable

- *Interests* – things that produce pleasure or satisfaction, but about which they can be flexible.

Helping people to discover, and to distinguish between, their needs and interests is the starting point to resolving all disputes.

What might some of Phil's *needs and interests* be? To get his life back on track, to feel in control, to manage his outgoings (including his lawyer's costs), to find a job, to take the opportunity to work with his brother-in-law, to provide for his family, to regain his self-esteem, to repair his relationship with Jen and Terry.

And what about Jen and Terry? To save their business, to manage cash flow (including legal costs), to reduce stress levels, to have more family time.

Needs and interests may be driven by:

Fact
What has actually happened and what people expect to happen next.

Behaviour
How people have treated each other in the past and how they intend to treat them in the future.

Beliefs and values
People's beliefs, whether based on religion, ideology or personal values, form the basis for their judgment about what is important, good or bad.

People often find it difficult to talk about their beliefs and values and often fear that others will be suspicious or intolerant of them.

Identity
Most important to resolving any kind of dispute is people's sense of self, including their sense of what is vital to them in terms of physical and psychological survival.

What matters most?

The key to resolving any conflict or dispute is to discover what matters most to the people involved.

To move away from defending positions towards understanding needs and interests, the question that needs to be answered is, 'So, what's important to you about...?' this question can help to uncover the real concerns and motives and to find out what a person really needs to find a solution.

If we could ask Phil, 'So what's important to you about *getting the redundancy payment?*'

Phil might answer, 'What's important is *that I get back to work and have some money to live on in the meantime.*'

'And what's important to you *about the money, what specifically would you use it for?*'

'*Well, if I could get approx £10,000 I could use it to buy a refrigerated van that I've seen advertised.*'

'And what's important to you about *a refrigerated van?*'

'*Well, if I could buy a refrigerated van, I could join my brother-in-law's fish delivery business.*'

If we could ask Jen and Terry, 'So what's important to you about *fighting Phil's claim for redundancy?*'

Jen and Terry might answer, 'What's important to us is *that we keep the business afloat. Keeping money in the business and cash flow is important right now.*'

'*And what's important to you about cash flow?*'

'*Well, we have a lot of money tied up in stock and vans, but no spare cash.*'

Similarities and differences

What are we looking for in discovering needs and interests?

First of all we are looking for things that the people involved share in common with one another. For example, both Phil and Jen and Terry share a wish to put the redundancy matter behind them and get on with their lives. Both need to manage their resources carefully and to be able to make a living in the future.

When people get right down to the bare necessities of life we quite often want exactly the same things and have the same fundamental needs – a job, a life, somewhere to live etc.

Finding common needs and interests can help people to understand each other better and relate to each other as caring humans, rather than as faceless adversaries.

Secondly, we are looking for differences that can be used to trade with; things that can add value for one person, but cost less for the other person to give.

Phil's most obvious need at this time is for a refrigerated van so that he can join his brother-in-law in business, but he does not have the cash to buy one.

Jen and Terry's most obvious need is to manage cash flow, however, they do have a fleet of redundant refrigerated vans.

Perhaps there is a possibility that Phil would take one of their refrigerated vans in settlement of his claim instead of cash?

Fears and concerns

The desire to succeed or to 'win' often dominates the thoughts, behaviour and actions of people in dispute.

For most of us winning means getting what we want, but determining what people really want is not as easy as it sounds. What a party claims to want may be very different from what they actually *need*.

In a legal dispute, a person may claim a sum of money when what they really need is to be acknowledged and understood as a human being; to know that their feelings, beliefs and values, their perception of the situation is valid.

The money claimed is important, but it may be less important than the values it represents.

People need to prove that they are right for the same reason that they get angry and threaten to publish a damning story in the press. They are afraid and what they fear most about being proved wrong is that they personally will somehow be worth less in the eyes of others.

Fear of failure is more about being unable to fulfil the expectations of ourselves and others and the impact that this has on our self-image. It is a fear of losing face rather than a fear of not accomplishing the task or acquiring the object that we so wanted.

'Winning' therefore is not always about attaining or acquiring what we want but about discovering what it is that we really need.

Hope against the odds

Let me tell you the story of a dispute[2]:

Mary Odds was a single mother with a large family. One of her sons, Danny, was a drug addict and after many years of injecting himself, the site of one of his injections became infected.

Danny visited his GP and was prescribed some antibiotics and the infection seemed to clear. His leg then became swollen and he was visited by an out-of-hours doctor who sent him to the hospital. At the hospital, they diagnosed a blood clot in his leg, and started treatment. Unfortunately, the diagnosis was wrong, Danny was subsequently found to have severe blood poisoning, by which time it was too late to save him and, very sadly, he died.

Mary Odds was full of grief, but also very angry and decided to sue Hopevale Hospital for the error in diagnosis. She consulted a lawyer who advised her that she had a strong case. She also spoke with a national newspaper and with a local radio station to discuss publishing the story and naming and shaming the hospital.

The legal case was started by the lawyers and the expensive job of preparing the case for trial began. After a while, however, it was suggested that the parties might be

[2] Based on a true case, but the names are fictitious.

prepared to work with a mediator to see if a settlement could be reached outside court.

Mrs Odds' position was that the hospital was negligent, the doctor had misdiagnosed Danny's illness and, as a result, he had died. She was claiming a substantial sum of money in compensation and her lawyer had advised her that she had a very good chance of winning in court.

Hopevale's position was that the doctor had made the correct diagnosis at the time, because all the evidence pointed to a blood clot and that any other doctor would have made the same decision. Their lawyer also advised that they had a very good chance of winning in court.

By relying only on their positions and the possibility of 'winning', it was impossible for Mrs Odds and Hopevale to move any closer to resolving their dispute.

What came out in the mediation, however, was that, apart from the misdiagnosis, which was not clear-cut, there were several factors in Danny's treatment that added to Mrs Odds' sense of anger.

In particular, she felt that the doctors and nurses looking after Danny were nervous about treating a known drug user and had been afraid of approaching him when his drugs started to wear off and he became abusive.

She felt very strongly that they needed to know how exactly to treat a similar patient in the future. What had really broken down was the relationship with the patient and his family because of fear and lack of knowledge and experience.

The outcome to this case was that both the hospital and Mrs Odds needed more than to agree over a sum of money to be paid. What was more important was to make sure that if such a situation should happen in the future the hospital would be prepared to deal with it; that the staff would have the skills to manage the patient and any relatives. Mrs Odds also needed the hospital to apologise for its failings.

Often when a family loses someone they love, they feel a *need* to do something positive in their memory. Sometimes they set up a trust or a charity. Mrs Odds found a far more creative solution that met both her *own need* to do something in memory of her son and the *hospital's need* to learn from past mistakes. She offered her services to the hospital to become their first Champion for drug users, a role that involved her in teaching the medical staff of the particular problems and requirements of a drug user entering hospital for treatment.

Experimenting with new positions

As we grow older and wiser, we also become fixed in our views. We see things from our own perspective, whether in terms of values, beliefs or ideas. As our minds become fixed, so do our bodies; we come stiffer and more rigid.

Yoga encourages me to stretch my body in ways that I would not normally contemplate, it challenges me to try new positions, gives me flexibility and helps me to see things from a different perspective – it quite literally enables me to turn my world upside down!

The other day, a new member joined our yoga class. Anna, our very lithe and supple teacher, helped him as much as possible with some of the more difficult poses. We then got to the bit in the evening where the entire class turns itself upside down. That's it: we literally stand on our heads for a few minutes.

It's amazing how different the world looks up the other way and how different people look with their noses so close to the floor.

John, our newcomer, decided he would try the headstand and despite his lack of practice, he was helped to turn his toes skywards and rather like a sky scraper in a hurricane he swayed there precariously for a while until eventually Anna said to the class, 'Well done, you can all come down now.'

Some of us descended gracefully to ground level and a few with more of a thud as Anna waited to start the next pose, but John continued to sway there until eventually he pleaded, 'Can someone tell me how to get down?' and another member of the class quickly responded, 'Oh, but that's next week's lesson!'

The moral of this story is that if we feel sufficiently supported, we can experiment with new positions. We can try experiencing life from a totally different place and begin to understand why others do not see the world and specific problems in exactly the same way that we do. We can begin to see that other people's needs and interests, fears and concerns are every bit as important as our own and that finding ways to acknowledge and meet them is far more important than 'winning'.

In a nutshell

Discovering each person's needs, interests, fears and concerns is more important than fighting to disprove their position on an issue. People need to be supported to face their fears and look at the world and the problem from a different perspective.

"Extreme positions are not succeeded by moderate ones, but by contrary extreme positions."
— **Friedrich Nietzsche**

6: WHAT SEX IS YOUR BRAIN?

How hormones affect how our brain is wired and how we respond to conflict

> *"15 per cent to 20 per cent of men have feminised brains. About 10 per cent of women have masculinised brains."*
>
> — Allan and Barbara Pease

BEDLAM
IN THE BOARDROOM

Finance Director, Dan, is going through a project proposal and budget with Geraldine. He is totally focused on the computer screen in front of them pulling up graphs and charts to illustrate how he predicts the new IT project will impact on corporate finances.

Geraldine, the IT director, is trying to have a conversation with Dan about who would be the best person to manage the project. She is looking for someone who will understand all the different personalities involved and the very real impact that the project will have on the business on a day-to-day basis.

'How do you feel that Peter would manage the project, Dan? Do you feel that he would handle the team well and get Phil and Ewan working well together?'

Without looking up from his screen Dan says, 'Yeah, fine. I think it all depends on if we can meet the budget in Q1 – see here...' he says, pointing at the model on the screen.

BEDROOM
BOREDOM IN THE

The next day Geraldine and her partner, John, are driving to a wedding. John is driving and Geraldine is map reading. It soon becomes clear that they are not on the right road. John becomes angry and asks Geraldine why she cannot read a simple map.

Geraldine is furious and replies, 'There is absolutely nothing wrong with my map reading! The trouble is that you were not listening properly and so you missed the last turn.'

They continue in this manner of reproach and denial until Geraldine says, 'Why don't we stop and just ask someone the way?' John ignores her and they continue in stony silence.

What happened? Why are Geraldine and John on different wavelengths when it comes to communicating about their journey?

Brain development

Women can't read maps; men don't listen.

Men love gadgets, facts and figures; women focus on relationships and conversation.

Where do these stereotypes for men and women come from? What impact do they have on our everyday lives at work and at home?

There has been an explosion of research into the way male and female brains work. We now know that the human brain has evolved over millions of years into the complex organ we have today.

Our brains are programmed primarily by the drive to survive. As humans we slowly evolved by a process of natural selection. Each change to our brains and bodies is the result of having to survive the continued battle for existence against other species and the environment.

The human brain is thought to have evolved in three stages:

The Reptilian Brain:

- The oldest and most primitive part, which is largely unchanged by evolution. This part of the brain controls body functions required for sustaining life such as breathing and body temperature. Behaviour originally determined by instinct, such as sex or defence of territory, may be driven by the Reptilian Brain.

The Mammalian Brain:

- The automatic control of body functions such as digestion, fluid balance, body temperature and blood pressure (Autonomic Nervous System, Hypothalamus).

- Filing new experiences as they happen and so creating a store of experience-based memories (Hippocampus).

- Experience-based recognition of danger and responding to this according to past experience, and some conscious feelings about events (Amygdala).

The development of the Mammalian Brain created a higher level of consciousness and enabled behaviour to be less rigidly controlled by pure instinct. Feelings such as attachment, anger and fear have emerged with associated behavioural responses. The fight or flight response is an example.

The Human Brain:

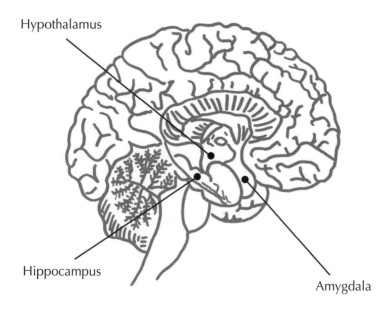

- Grey matter called the Neocortex envelopes most of the earlier brain and amounts to about 85 per cent of the human brain mass.

- The Neocortex is divided into two hemispheres, left and right, which are separated, but able to communicate with each other.

Left or right?

Are you more right brained or left brained?

Just as you have a dominant hand, dominant eye, and even a dominant foot, you probably have a dominant side of the brain. People who are left-handed tend to have a bias towards the right hemisphere, which is the creative side of the brain. For example, Albert Einstein, Leonardo Da Vinci and Picasso were all left-handed.

While brain research confirms that both sides of the brain are involved in nearly every human activity, we do know that the left side of the brain is the seat of language and processes in a logical and sequential order. The right side is more visual and processes intuitively, holistically and randomly.

Brain functions

LEFT	Right
uses logic	uses feeling
detail oriented	'big picture' oriented
facts rule	imagination rules
words and language	symbols and images
present and past	present and future
math and science	philosophy and religion
can comprehend	can 'get it' (i.e. meaning)
knowing	believes
acknowledges	appreciates
order/pattern perception	spatial perception
knows object name	knows object function
reality based	fantasy based
forms strategies	presents possibilities
practical	impetuous
safe	risk taking

Our brains are contra lateral, meaning that the left hemisphere controls the movement of the right side of our body and the right hemisphere controls the left side of our body. A left-handed person will, therefore, be right brain dominant while a right-handed person will be left brain dominant.

What sex is your brain?

Fiona is on the phone to her mother discussing plans for a family party at the weekend. With the phone tucked under her ear, she is also chopping vegetables for the family's evening meal and at the same time glancing at her son's homework diary that he has just thrust under her nose, making a mental note as she does so that he must tackle his algebra tonight.

George, Fiona's husband, wanders in with a glass of wine in his hand. He overhears Fiona discussing with her mother the arrangements, where everyone will sleep, what food to cook for Phoebe, the vegetarian sister-in-law, what to do if Uncle Henry gets drunk! When the phone conversation ends, George switches straight into problem-solving mode, 'What you need to do,' he says 'is...'

Why is it that men love to solve problems and know how things work, but are wary of emotion, and that women are better at interpersonal relationships, can read emotions and can multi-task?

Recent research into brain sex has discovered that there may be a simple explanation for some of the stereo-typical differences between male and female behaviour. While most people display a preference between right and left handedness and the traits linked with dominant use of the right or left side of the brain scientists have now discovered a link between hand preference and sexuality.

It's thought that testosterone plays an important role in the way we think and behave and that that exposure to testosterone in the womb may play a role in determining both handedness and sexual orientation.

The theory is that exposure to high levels of testosterone is linked with more assertive behaviour, with problem solving and with creating systems. In other words, men like to get deeply involved in activities such as car repair, computing or building up an extensive music collection and they love to discover the rules that govern a system.

Exposure to lower levels of testosterone is linked to more nurturing behaviour, to relationship building and empathy. In other words, women are likely to be better at guessing other people's emotions and responding appropriately.

An 'extreme male brain', one that is very good at creating systems but very poor at empathy, which affects more men than women, may be linked to exposure to abnormally high levels of testosterone.

Brain sex is not an absolute and each of us falls somewhere along a spectrum between extreme male and extreme female. Having a more systematic brain does not necessarily mean that you are a male any more than being more empathic means you are a female, it simply determines the way your brain works.

People whose brains are wired mainly for feminine thinking are more likely to make decisions and deal with problems based on intuition or gut feeling and are more likely to be creative and insightful. People whose brains are wired mainly for masculine thinking are likely to make decisions and deal with problems using statistical data, logic and analysis with their emotions hardly influencing them at all.

So what sex is your brain? Various tests exist to help you determine your own brain sex. Go to http://www.bbc.co.uk/science/humanbody/sex/add_user.shtml on the BBC website or you can measure your fingers.

Fig 6.1

Finger length

Some scientists [1] believe that the ratio of index finger length to ring finger length indicates how much testosterone we were exposed to in our mother's womb.

If the ring finger is longer than the index finger, it is likely that the person was exposed to more testosterone in the womb.

Finger ratios are calculated simply by measuring the index finger of the right hand, then the ring finger, and dividing the former by the latter. Those with a longer ring finger have a ratio of less than 1. This is called the 'Casanova pattern'. Those with higher, or more feminised ratios, will have ratios greater than 1. The average ratio for men is 0.98.

On average, women's index and ring fingers are almost equal in length because they are exposed to less testosterone. In men, the ring finger tends to be longer because they have higher testosterone levels. In general, women exposed to more testosterone have more 'masculine hands' – i.e. longer ring fingers.

Can you change?

Have you now discovered what sex your brain is and where you sit on the right/left brain spectrum? If so, what can you do about it and can you change?

[1] The Finger Book by John Manning

Knowing how your brain is wired is one of the easiest psychological profiling tools to use and understand. The first benefit is self-knowledge, knowing why we prefer to focus on certain types of information and resist or ignore others. The second advantage is that of understanding others and realising that they may have a different way of thinking, rather than simply being disrespectful of what's important to us.

This knowledge also helps us to focus on practising and improving our use of the side of the brain we prefer to use least.

Here are some things you can do:

If you are predominately Right Brain then to develop your Left Brain:

- Fill in the details – if you think in big pictures be methodical in filling in the fine details of whatever you're working on

- Tidy up – find a place for everything and keep it there. Right Brain people tend to be more messy

- Read a map – plan a cross country orienteering expedition plotting map references

- Plot your family tree – draw a picture of your family tree with names and dates of birth and death of all your relatives.

If you are predominately Left Brain then to develop your Right Brain:

- Become an artist – learn to draw or play a musical instrument

- Daydream – spend time creating a vision of some time or event in the future

- Meditate – learn to meditate and switch off your chattering Left Brain altogether

- Remember your dreams – first thing in the morning before you leap out of bed and engage with your left brain; make an effort to recall the dream you were having when you awoke.

Whatever you are working on in the office or at home, logic, analysis and statistics should be interspersed with feelings, emotions, metaphors and jokes. Use stories, gestures, descriptions and pictures in your communications with others. Play games, laugh and be joyful.

> *"He who laughs last doesn't get it."*
> — Helen Giangregorid

Male/female dispute resolution

Most formal processes for resolving disputes focus on left brain skills and tools, reliance on evidence and facts, words and language, logical argument, judgment etc. Less formal processes of resolution are open to the use of more right brain skills and tools such as creative problem solving, empathy, listening and big picture thinking.

Henry and Juliet were in dispute with their builder. During the building of an extension for Juliet's elderly parents to live in, there were so many problems and allegations of sub-standard workmanship and poor quality materials that Juliet's parents were forced to live in a caravan at the end of the garden for two months after selling their own home.

The final straw came when they eventually moved in and it was discovered that the boiler was defective and might have caused them serious harm. Henry was furious, Steve, the builder, had been a friend of his for many years and they had plans to work on some other building schemes together.

Despite their friendship, Henry issued legal proceedings against Steve in an effort to achieve 'justice' and some compensation for all the hardship and emotional turmoil

> *they had to go through, as well as the cost of putting everything right. But, as Henry read through the growing file of legal papers and letters all he could see were schedules of facts and figures and experts reports and nothing that dealt with the real problem between him and Steve.*
>
> *Eventually a friend suggested to Henry that he might try mediation as a less formal way of dealing with his problem with Steve.*
>
> *On the day of the mediation, Henry was fascinated as the need to focus on facts and figures and legal rights and wrongs was balanced with a feeling that his story was being listened to for the first time, and a discovery that empathy and understanding as well as money might be part of the solution. Finally, Henry and Steve were able to shake hands and share a glass of wine together while tentatively discussing plans for working together again.*

Combining the skills and tools of right and left brain thinking can provide us with many more options for understanding and managing conflicts and disputes in a totally different way.

Mars and Venus

Once we understand that there may be fundamental differences between the male and female brain we are empowered to use this vital information in our dealings with others, whether at work or at home.

Those of us that fall on the female side of the brain sex spectrum know that our male-brained counterparts are not deliberately lacking in empathy. Their masculine priorities can lead them to focus on power, systems and facts rather than feelings, teamwork and collaboration.

Those of us on the male side of the brain sex spectrum know that our female-brained counterparts are not deliberately ignoring the logic or our argument or being unappreciative of our efforts to solve their problems. However, they do need us to engage with their emotions and demonstrate the value of relationships.

As with Geraldine and Dan and Geraldine and John, relationships disintegrate when we fail to acknowledge and appreciate that we are biologically different and blame each other for not living up to our own male- or female-brained expectations.

Most organisations today are embracing feminine values in the way they manage relationships with co-workers, customers and suppliers. Meanwhile they are still demonstrating the traditional masculine values that drive the desire for success and domination in the market place.

Families can also benefit from parents who seek to establish a truce between the sexes and help each other to develop an approach to relationships and problem solving that makes allowances for, as well as cherishes and values, the biological differences between us.

In a nutshell

Each of us falls somewhere on a spectrum between extreme male and extreme female brain.

Our values, attitudes and behaviour are affected by our biologically determined brain sex.

We need to both acknowledge and appreciate these differences in our dealings with one another at work and at home.

> "The main difference between men and women is that men are lunatics and women are idiots."
> — Rebecca West

7: LOVE MATTERS

Why love and fear are at the heart of most conflicts

> *"One word frees us of all the weight and pain of life: That word is love."*
>
> — Sophocles (496–406 BC)

BEDLAM
IN THE BOARDROOM

Fiona is the only female on the board of directors. Godfrey, the CEO, is a bully. In front of the other directors, he belittles and embarrasses Fiona, ignores her contributions in meetings and responds with, 'There, there, dear,' when she objects. Team building and client events such as visits to rugby matches are organised deliberately to exclude her. Godfrey's focus is entirely on himself, his achievements, his wealth and his possessions. Feisty Fiona is tired of fighting her corner and decides to leave.

BEDROOM
BOREDOM IN THE

Godfrey's wife, Deirdre, is furious with him. He was a total embarrassment at the dinner party last night, drinking too much and telling stories of his youthful escapades that were not at all amusing to the (female) guests. Godfrey is not entirely sure what he has done wrong, but he does know that he had better keep a low profile for a while if he is to avoid further repercussions!

Love and fear

Godfrey has upset both his fellow director, Fiona, and his wife, Deirdre. So what's love got to do with it? Why might love and fear be at the heart of both of these conflicts?

Love and fear are the two principle states of mind:

Fiona is angry with Godfrey, but she is also scared. She's scared that her fellow directors do not think highly enough of her or respect her achievements.

Behind his bullying façade, Godfrey is also worried. He is worried that Fiona is smarter than he is and that he will be shown up as a weak CEO unless he emphasises his higher status.

Deirdre is furious, but she is also jealous of the attention that Godfrey was paying to the other female guests at dinner. Jealousy is also a form of fear, because you are afraid that you are inferior to other people.

So anger, jealousy, worry and depression are all expressions of fear.

What we are usually most afraid of is that other people do not love and respect us enough.

So when we get angry with another person, our anger is often a mask for other feelings.

If Deirdre's son, Jamie, is late home Deirdre is angry, but she is also scared because she thought that Jamie was hurt.

Perhaps Fiona is worried about losing her job. She may be afraid that she won't find another job and afraid that she won't be able to pay the bills.

If we are able to understand and acknowledge the *fear* then instead of getting angry, we can attempt to explain our feelings.

'I was terrified that something had happened to you.'

'I was afraid that we would not have enough money to pay the mortgage.'

And often what we really want to say is,

'I was scared that you didn't *love* me anymore.'

Ego

Why does it bother us if someone gets angry with us or if they reject or ignore us?

What is it that is behind our own anger, desire for revenge or need to 'put the record straight' by proving that we are right and they are wrong?

The reason is that when someone gets angry it is usually because he is *afraid* – he is afraid that he has lost control of his fragile image of himself. Anger is his instinctive response to fear.

The impact of the behaviour of another person towards us depends not on what they did, but on how we feel about it. How we feel about another's behaviour depends to a great degree on how we feel about ourselves.

Self-esteem is literally how we *feel* about ourselves.

In order to be happy, to have good relationships and be psychologically balanced, we need to feel good about ourselves. We literally need to love ourselves. This self-love is called self-esteem.

Self-esteem can be gained only through self-respect, because you have to respect yourself to be able to love yourself.

If you do or say something and the motivation is to make you look or feel good, rather than because it is the right thing to do, then you will not respect yourself.

On a recent holiday, I shared a chalet with Paul. Paul had built a successful business and reputation and he wanted to keep reminding us of it. Every evening at dinner, the conversation would be dominated by Paul's jokes and stories, by Paul's opinion on everything we discussed and by details of his numerous cars, homes and possessions. It got to the stage where when the other guests saw Paul coming someone would whisper, 'The Ego has landed'.

Paul appeared to have a very high opinion of himself, but, in reality it was like a tower of cards and Paul was terrified that someone would blow and make them all collapse.

People with low self-esteem are extremely sensitive and fragile, always seeking to impress others and alert for signs of approval and respect.

If we have low self-respect and therefore low self-esteem we are constantly seeking signs of love and respect from others to help us fill a gap.

The part of us that seeks love and respect from others is called the ego.

If we have low self-esteem and someone is rude or angry towards us we will automatically interpret their behaviour as a sign of disrespect.

Sense of self

Our sense of self is linked to three major nervous systems:

- Autonomic – feelings

- Somatic – physical actions

- Central

  - verbal – conceptual thinking
  - non-verbal – visual thinking

We develop feelings about ourselves.

We anticipate our ability to take effective action.

We develop thoughts about ourselves.

These internal experiences of one's self are referred to as:

- Self-esteem

- Self-confidence

- Self-concept.

When these are strong, positive and healthy, you can cope well with work, relationships and with life's adversities.

If your inner resources are not strong, you tend to suffer more and cope less well.

Self-esteem

> *Godfrey hopes that he will impress the dinner party guests with his stories and perhaps he also hopes that Fiona will be impressed by his macho image and superiority at work.*

Self-esteem is your emotional opinion of yourself – how you feel about yourself as a person.

Job-title, pay cheque or social standing are external proofs of importance, but they are **not** *the real source* of anyone's self-esteem.

People with weak self-esteem often exaggerate or cling to external proofs to compensate for lack of self-esteem.

People with strong self-esteem feel less vulnerable to the negative opinions of others and are less likely to end up in unnecessary conflict.

Self-confidence

A new IT system is being introduced at work and Godfrey is terrified that he will not get to grips with it. Perhaps his bullish behaviour is designed to deflect his co-director's attention from this fact.

People lacking self-confidence feel they cannot rely on themselves and so they avoid risky situations – they suffer a great deal when thrown into a situation that requires them to perform unfamiliar tasks or navigate unknown territory. Godfrey is concerned that he will make a fool of himself and is trying to find the means to avoid the issue that will create this situation.

People with strong self-confidence know they can count on themselves more than they can count on anyone else. They expect to handle adversities and to succeed in new activities. If Godfrey were to talk to the people installing the system and ask them for tips, he could be open that it's new territory for him. Also he might suggest that he will not be the only person with this learning curve to climb and find he can share the learning process.

Self-concept

Fiona has a high-powered job and is one of only a handful of female directors in similar positions. She has an impressive list of contacts, dresses in designer suits and eats at smart restaurants. Losing her position on the board would be a big deal for her.

Self-concept refers to your idea about who or what you are.

Some of your self-concept is based on your occupation or employment; many people who lose their jobs have a difficult time, because their identities have been based on their work. Fiona has high self-esteem and high self-confidence – now her self-concept is being challenged she will need to revise her thoughts about herself.

For some people, the need for self-concept is so strong that they will lie about what they have accomplished and how much they earn. If Fiona finds her position and power threatened she could choose one of two routes – deny the issue and pretend she still holds her high-powered position or use her powerful approach to find herself a new, better position. Her choice may depend on her core values and how much self-esteem and confidence she has in herself.

Some people try to compensate for a weak self-concept with impressive clothing, titles, high income, important friends, the right address, outstanding children and other external proofs of success.

That is why they are so devastated when they lose their external proofs and why Fiona may fear the loss of her job and all that goes with it.

Trust and respect

Where does our sense of self come from? What is it that determines whether we interpret a disagreement with a colleague as a deliberate attempt to undermine us or a misunderstanding to be resolved?

It is as though each of us has an invisible antennae testing for signals that others trust and respect us. Every human is conducting a moment-to-moment test for trust and respect by checking

- *Do I matter?* and

- *Am I heard?*

If, in our communications with others, we feel that our needs, interests, fears and concerns have been acknowledged and understood then we will sense that we do matter and that we *have* been heard. When this happens we are more likely to co-operate with others in resolving any problem or conflict.

On the other hand, if we feel that our needs, interests, fears and concerns have not been acknowledged and understood, we will sense that we *do not matter* and that we *are not heard*. When this happens we may sabotage any attempts to resolve any problem or conflict.

> *Fiona has an issue with her secretary, Dawn. She has noticed that Dawn often arrives five or ten minutes late for work. Fiona has reprimanded Dawn many times and explained that it doesn't reflect well on the company if she is not answering her phone after the office has opened.*
>
> *Fiona says to Dawn, 'You are an excellent secretary and I really appreciate the way that you use your initiative, welcome clients and are so efficient. I understand that you have a small child to get to nursery in the mornings and that may sometimes be difficult for you. Could I ask you to help me with something please...*

Fiona is starting the process of building trust and respect by acknowledging Dawn's needs, interests and concerns.

> *Godfrey is angry with his colleague, Ben, who keeps parking in his car parking space rather than walking around the corner to his own. Godfrey bumps into Ben in reception and immediately launches into a tirade, 'I cannot believe how lazy you are, Ben, you just cannot be bothered to walk the extra distance. It just goes to show that you are not a team player...'*

Godfrey is starting the process of creating a rift in the workplace – which will almost certainly affect their ability to work together.

Why is Fiona's reaction to a disagreement with a work colleague so different to Godfrey's?

Our feelings and reactions to conflict may relate back to the earliest years of our life. Early love and care actually shapes the nervous system and determines how conflict is interpreted and responded to in adulthood.

If, as a baby and in childhood, we did not receive unconditional love and affection from our parents, perhaps due to an alcoholic or depressed mother or father, we are likely to have experienced feelings of fear and anxiety.

I remember clearly a child at my daughter's primary school, who came from an unhappy home, constantly asking her teachers, classmates and visiting parents 'Do you love me? Do you love me?' and having to beg her mother every day 'Promise to pick me up, Mum? You do promise, don't you?'

Such children are likely to grow up as adults with very low self-esteem, desperate for love and attention. They may interpret expressions of anger or unhappiness as signs that they are unloved and disrespected and react instinctively causing a cycle of blame and conflict that is difficult to break.

The key principle to remember is that every human's moment-to-moment test for trust and respect is

Do I *matter?*

Am I *heard?*

Reach out and touch

On a chilly Sunday afternoon Bethany was shopping in Manhattan's Union Square when she spotted a man standing on the sidewalk dressed in a hooded sweatshirt holding a sign, his hands shaking from the cold.

He wasn't asking for money, food or a job. In fact, he had something to give. His sign had two simple words on it: FREE HUGS.

Bethany put down her shopping bags and gave the man, Andy, a warm embrace.

Kathy Sykes, Professor of Sciences and Society at the University of Bristol, has investigated the effectiveness of reflexology and other alternative therapies. Professor Sykes found evidence that reflexology does work to help people in pain and discomfort.

The key of both hugs and reflexology is the power of touch. As humans we value human contact. Being touched with care and compassion can sooth, calm and heal.

People can be touched by a kind word, a smile or a gesture in the same way as a hug.

When we know that people in conflict are longing for a sign that they are loved and respected and we can show them that as fellow humans they matter and we care then we have taken the first and most important step to resolution.

If only we could remember that human worth is not proportionate to human achievement. It simply cannot be measured in talent, position, age, wealth, role, belongings and trophies. It cannot be measured by power or status or by winning or losing whether in sport or in the commercial arena.

The value of human life is beyond measure. Every person is invaluable and deserves all possible respect and love – not for anything that he or she has achieved but simply by virtue of being human.

In a nutshell

Understand that love and fear are at the heart of most conflicts.

Learn to give love, respect, care and attention to others even when you are in disagreement.

> *"The world will be a better place when the power of love replaces the love of power."*
>
> — William E Gladstone

8: WINNERS
AND LOSERS

Why winning is not always all that we dreamed of

> "f you can meet with triumph and disaster and treat those two impostors just the same."
>
> — Rudyard Kipling

BEDLAM IN THE BOARDROOM

Jim's father, Arthur, was the Chairman of the family company. For as long as he could remember, Jim was going to join the company and eventually take over the business from his father. During school and university holidays Jim worked at the company and, as soon as he graduated, he joined the staff as a sales manager. He quickly worked his way up to a seat on the board.

When Arthur celebrated his 65th birthday, Jim waited for him to speak of plans for his retirement, he began to think about changes he would make to transform the business and modernise the offices, but no such plans were spoken of. By the time Arthur reached the age of 70 Jim was celebrating his 40th birthday. He began to resent his father's continued presence at the office and desire to cling to power.

Jim began to plot and scheme with the other directors to 'persuade' Arthur to retire. He conspired with his mother, Jill, to beg Arthur to spend more time at home with her. Then all of a sudden and without warning, Arthur stepped down on his 75th birthday and Jim at last, assumed the role of Chairman.

Three months later sitting in his new office Jim wondered what all the fuss had been about. His lifelong dream had been to take over the company from his father and now after all the wishing and hoping, planning and conniving, he doesn't feel as pleased and proud as he thought he would with what he has achieved.

BEDROOM

BOREDOM IN THE

Jim and his wife, Celia, are getting divorced. Celia is tired of all the family politics and endless focus on the business. After years of supporting Jim as he waited for the top job, Celia feels cast aside and ignored as Jim spends more and more time at the office and, instead of being happy at achieving his long held dream, seems to be withdrawn and depressed.

They have each hired a top legal team to represent them in their fight. Celia is determined to *win* custody of the children and a substantial pay-out from Jim in order to get her revenge.

Jim is determined to *win* by proving that his assets and the business are not worth as much as Celia claims, getting his pay-back for having to move out of their grand family home.

Next door

Christopher and Emily are sad that their marriage is over. They have agreed to hire collaborative lawyers with the intention of agreeing between them the best childcare and financial arrangements. After seven years of marriage, they hope that they can retain their friendship with one another and together help the children to come to terms with the change in arrangements.

Who are the 'winners' here? Why is winning so important to us? And why does it so often fail to live up to our expectations?

Why do you want to win?

The desire to win, whether a sporting competition, a business deal, or an argument, is rooted in the evolutionary need to survive.

The fight or flight response primes us to react instinctively to immediate threats. It is designed to protect us from danger and death and creates both alertness and fear that prompt us to act in self-preservation.

Brian thinks he hears a burglar enter his house in the middle of the night. Geraldine hears footsteps behind her while walking home from the station in the dark. Perceiving a threat, their bodies produce a surge of adrenaline, triggering a cascade of stress hormones that give them a critical boost of energy and strength to enable them to run or attack.

The butterflies we feel in our stomach before an important interview or the dry mouth we experience before we make a speech are the result of the *same instinctive* reaction to threat.

We want to win because we are programmed to survive.

> *Imagine that you are stranded in shark infested waters with just a life raft to hang on to. After several hours you begin to give up hope of being rescued; you are cold and thirsty; you can feel your energy draining away.*
>
> *You begin to feel hopeless, what if no one comes?*
>
> *Then, you think you can hear a helicopter, and gradually it gets closer and closer until it is circling overhead. With a jerk, your energy is back you wave and scream. At that precise moment, you feel you could climb any mountain, overcome any challenge.*
>
> *Without warning, the helicopter turns and flies away again. Your bubble of energy is burst and you can barely raise an ounce of motivation to continue moving your limbs in an effort to survive.*

The desire to win gives us the energy and the motivation to survive in an emergency or a crisis.

But where does the sustained drive and motivation to pursue a desire to win come from?

Risk and reward

What motivates someone to pursue a goal, a desire, or a dream for months and years?

Dopamine is a brain chemical that gives you a natural high. It creates feelings of pleasure or euphoria that keep you coming back for more. When we take a risk and we are successful the brain reacts to the unexpected reward by releasing dopamine. The feeling of euphoria acts as a positive reinforcement that encourages us to keep taking risks.

Once the brain has received a dopamine buzz it then begins to predict situations in which it will get more of a high. Russian physiologist, Ivan Pavlov, would ring a bell whenever his laboratory dogs were about to be fed. After a while, they learnt to associate the sound of the bell with the arrival of their food and would begin to salivate before their food even arrived. In the same way, people who have been rewarded once begin to predict future gains or wins and the brain releases dopamine in response to the anticipation.

Flooding the brain with dopamine at the very thought of winning is what keeps people motivated to carry on. When we are in conflict, it is the vision we create of winning, of being proved right or of getting even with our opponent that spurs us on. It is the same *vision of winning* that keeps athletes training in the cold dark nights of winter, actors rehearsing in anticipation of the curtain call and staff motivated to work overtime on a project.

If people have a strong vision of the goal and the experience of previous success, dopamine release will keep their drive and determination on a high for a long period of time.

A team led by Harvard's Hans Breiter found a striking similarity between the brains of people trying to predict financial rewards and the brains of cocaine addicts and morphine users. In effect, we get stoned on our own belief that we know what's coming. As time passes, we may get more of a dopamine high from predicting a coming gain than from earning the gain itself.

But what if we don't win?

> Manchester United beats Chelsea in the European Cup. The fans go wild; the players are euphoric; the manager is proud; this is the moment of his dreams. The losing team on the other hand are dejected. Some break down and cry, this match was nearly theirs, but it slipped away in the closing moments. If only they could rewind the clock and replay the penalty shoot out. They do – over and over in their minds.
>
> The Oxford and Cambridge boat race has just finished. The teams are slumped exhausted over their oars. The winning team revive quickly to celebrate their win and face the press. The losing team can barely lift their heads. Every minute of every day this last year has been focused on this race; on this moment. Training schedules, social diary, diet and nutrition, support of family and friends. Everything designed to achieve just one result.

So it appears that if the win fails to materialise or to meet your expectation your dopamine dries up *instantly*. This creates a wrenching swing from euphoria to depression – which can take place in less than two seconds.

This phenomenon may also explain the anticlimax we sometimes experience on achieving a long cherished goal.

Jim has dreamed for so long of taking over the family business from his father and now that he has what he wanted, the reality does not live up to his expectations. His subsequent depression and withdrawal is the final straw for his long suffering wife, Celia.

It's as though, in the end, the journey to success was ultimately more rewarding than the destination.

What do you want to win?

When I ask people what outcome they hope for from their conflict or dispute rather than what they want to win, they are often stuck for an answer.

Winning in their minds is often about being proved right after a long legal fight, or obtaining justice, a matter of principle. However, this is before they have understood the difference between positions and needs and interests. Once we begin to explore below the surface of their dispute and to discover what's really important to them, 'winning' can start to take on a new meaning.

If we were to ask Jim what outcome he really wanted from his long-running conflict with his father about his role in the family business, he might reflect that status was important to him, that at the age of 40 he no longer wants to be seen as the office junior – so that it isn't the job of Chairman itself that he finds so attractive, but the effect that would have on his self-esteem. He might also like a better work/life balance and more quality time with his family, all of which have suffered as he has striven to gain what he thought he wanted.

What about Jim's father, Arthur? What is behind his desire to hold on to the role of company Chairman for so long? Perhaps there is an issue of status for him too or a dread of feeling useless after so long at the top. Maybe he is worried that Jim does not have all the skills he needs to help the company survive in a different world to when it was started.

Instead of a simple win/lose scenario it suddenly becomes possible to search for solutions that meet the needs and concerns of both Jim and

Arthur. A consultancy role for Arthur, management training for Jim, delegation of some tasks to free up time for Jim and his family – suddenly it is possible for both to win.

Wanting and needing to have things work out well for *everyone involved* is the focus of collaborative processes such as mediation. It is also a trait of the most successful survivors.

In his book, *The Survivor Personality*, Al Siebert describes people who automatically seek out opportunities to meet everyone's needs as being life's best survivors. Ruth Benedict, a cultural anthropologist, describes them as 'synergistic humans' She described a spectrum where at one end any act or skill that advantages the individual is at the expense of others, and at the other end any act or skill that advantages the individual at the same time advantages others.

Benedict used the term *Low Synergy* to describe acts that are mutually opposed and counteracted and *High Synergy* to describe acts that are mutually reinforcing.

Wanting and needing to have things work well for everyone requires you to have an accurate understanding of what people think and feel and of what is most important to them.

High Synergy is one of the most important skills for the 21st century as well as for resolving conflicts and disputes.

Is that all there is?

Rather like taking drugs, the high experienced by winning an argument needs to be repeated to be sustained.

Winning at this level is about power and making someone feel more powerful can have the effect of bolstering self-esteem. However, in general, it is only people with low self-esteem who need to win to feel good about themselves.

Power is lonely because it separates and isolates us from our fellow human beings. They may give in to our demands, but they may also fear or hate us for it. If we win the argument, but lose respect or love or being valued by others, the win is shallow and worthless.

In the end, whether you experience the euphoric highs and the crushing lows associated with winning and losing depends on the purpose behind the goal. If the purpose was simply to prove that you were right, if you were motivated by a desire for revenge or by a need for power, it is likely that your victory will be a hollow one. On the other hand, if you were motivated by a higher goal or grander destiny that is not linked to your own self-esteem, you will be far better equipped to meet the imposters of triumph and disaster.

How would it be if we did not have to deal with the highs and lows of winning and losing and the tensions of conflicts and disputes? What would we achieve then? The answer is probably not much.

We need the memories of past challenges won and the depressive anti-climax to spur us into action, to set out on new adventures and to seek to change the world for the better. These memories send us in search of a vision that is grander and more inspiring than our small and insignificant selves.

> Running the London Marathon is a personal achievement, but if I do it for a worthy charity with a host of supporters cheering me on, it's a different game.
>
> Scheming to be CEO of a pharmaceutical company because of the status it confers is a sad ambition compared to the desire to run the same company because of the fervent desire to help it to succeed, because it produces a medical product that can save the lives of children.

Argument and winning is, in fact, an art and not a sport – there is a technique and a mind-set to it – and the skill once learned can deliver far more satisfaction than the brutal and blunt effect of overpowering another person. Winning at this level is about getting what we want at the same time as helping others to get what they want.

Winning should be empowering *rather* than overpowering.

In a nutshell

Winning should be about getting what we need at the same time as helping others to get what they need.

"To travel hopefully is better than to arrive."

— Robert Louis Stevenson

9: THE ART OF TRUE CONVERSATION

Why we don't know how to speak and how to listen

> *"Most conversations are simply monologues delivered in the presence of witnesses."*
>
> — Margaret Miller

BEDLAM
IN THE BOARDROOM

Across the town parents are opening their morning mail. An ordinary looking letter from St Thomas's Girls School contains a shock announcement, 'The Governors have for some time been considering the future of the school and after much deliberation have decided that the school should become co-educational. The new intake of boys will begin next autumn.'

Some parents whose mail arrives late receive this news from their children, whose friends have already posted their thoughts on Facebook. The largely female staff are also unhappy, they had heard rumours that a change was being discussed, but no one had asked them what they thought or how they felt.

By 9.00 am on Monday the phones are already ringing, angry letters being delivered by parents dropping their children off for school and the staff room is alight with gossip. An emergency meeting of the Board of Governors is called.

BEDROOM
BOREDOM IN THE

Dorothy and Charles have travelled to work together every day for the last five years. Charles drives their trusty old red car and Dorothy sits in the passenger seat. Every day they take the same route and towards the end of their journey they have to cross a dual carriageway and join the traffic from the opposite direction. As they approach the tricky junction, Charles looks to the left and then says to Dorothy, 'Everything all right, dear?' 'Yes fine, dear' she replies, and they continue on their way.

Today they follow the same routine and as they reach the junction Charles says, 'Everything all right, dear?' and she says

'Yes fine, dear' but as Charles pulls out to cross the road he sees a large truck bearing down on them...

Later, as Dorothy and Charles wait at the hospital, he says to her, 'Every day when we get to that junction I ask you if it's all right to cross and you say, "Yes fine, dear"; didn't you see that truck was about to hit us?' and Dorothy replies, 'Every day when you said, "All right, dear?", I assumed that you were enquiring how I was today.'

Why listening matters

Did Dorothy hear what Charles said to her each and every day on their way to work? Yes, she did! Did she receive the meaning of his message? No, she did not. Dorothy assumed that Charles' message to her was about something totally different – her wellbeing first thing in the morning rather than the safety of the road ahead.

Why are the parents and staff at St Thomas's so angry and upset? They are angry and upset because no one thought to consult them about this important change. Even if the decision to go co-educational is the right long-term decision, their understanding and support would have been more forthcoming if they had felt *important* enough to have been consulted.

Whenever people are involved in a relationship and especially when they are in communication or conversation they are subconsciously conducting a test for trust and respect. The test is continuous, it happens from moment-to-moment and is based on what people see, hear or feel. As we established in Chapter 7, what they want to know more than anything else is 'Do I matter?' and 'Am I heard?'

Messages and meaning

When I tell you my story, what do you hear? Do you hear the story that I thought I was telling?

The most important thing to remember is this – the message that a person or an organisation intends to give in communicating with others is *frequently* not the message that the other receives.

The school governors may believe that they are delivering good news to the recipients of their letters. A decision has been made to ensure that the school is more likely to survive in the long term, but that is not the message that the parents and staff are receiving. For some, the message they receive is 'You were not important enough for us to take the time to listen to your views on this issue.'

Why is there so often a mismatch between the message we intended to deliver and the meaning that the other person actually gets? How is it that we can express ourselves with great clarity and still fail to communicate?

What are we listening for?

> Terry is late home from work. He did work late as he told his wife, Susan, but he also had a quick pint at the Duck and Drake with the rest of the team before heading home and now it is dark and way past dinner time.
>
> Susan has had a tough day and has been waiting for Terry to arrive home so that she could share the details and tell him about her difficult boss. Susan pours Terry a drink and launches into her story. Terry does not seem to be picking up on the detail; he hasn't even commented on the sarcastic comments about her performance that Susan says her boss has been making all day.

The trouble is that Terry is not really listening to her story. He *is* hearing the words that Susan is saying, but he is not hearing what is *important* to her. What Terry is listening for is a sign from Susan that he is forgiven for being so late. When Terry is late home without warning Susan is usually very angry and after the day that he has had the last thing that Terry needs now is an angry wife.

The fact is that when we are listening or supposed to be listening what we actually pay close attention to is the things that directly concern us – things which are relevant to our own situation, our own needs, interests, fears and concerns. Terry is *listening from his point of view*, not from Susan's.

The same is true when we are speaking, we believe that people will automatically understand what we are saying and get our message. We honestly believe that if only we can craft what we are saying in the right words, the most persuasive terms, then our listeners will immediately see things the way that we do and accept our point of view.

The truth is that unless **both** the speaker and the listener share the same meaning in the message then the words may be totally lost and meaningless.

The key to all communication

All communication is about creating understanding. A person who is speaking whether to a partner, colleague or to a group is saying to his or her listeners *please understand me*. On the other hand, a listener is saying to the speaker, 'I do not understand your message unless it is relevant to me; *please understand me*.'

So, the key, whether you are a speaker or a listener, is to *show that you understand* – to give a very clear indication that you are aware of and respectful of the other person's needs, interests, fears and concerns. That you can, even if only for a brief moment in time, stand in their shoes and see the world as they see it, rather than as you see it.

Instead of focusing on his own concerns, if Terry could really listen to the story that Susan is trying to tell him he could show his understanding by saying, ' I can see that you're frustrated that I'm late home and it sounds as though you've had a difficult day at work...'

For her part, Susan needs to acknowledge where Terry is coming from before launching into her story. She might start by saying something like, 'It looks as though you've had a long day and I guess that you've had a quick drink in the pub on the way home, my day has been pretty tough too...'

If you can do this then the person that you are communicating with will begin to have trust in you. They will want to share information with you and join with you in either a conversation or a relationship. If you cannot demonstrate understanding then the end result may be that the other person will resist your efforts at communication and seek to undermine and avoid conversation and a deeper relationship with you.

Empathy

Penny arrives home from work, tired and hungry, to find the kitchen bin overflowing. When her husband, Ben, arrives back a short while later Penny accosts him with a raised voice, 'Why don't you ever take the rubbish out?' Ben stares at the newspaper and replies, 'Penny, that is wrong. I remember quite clearly taking the rubbish out last Wednesday at 9 pm and on the Wednesday before that, the 10th, at exactly the same time.'

Like many couples, Penny and Ben are locked in an exchange where the emotion felt by one person is being met with the logical argument of the other. Penny is focused on the *emotional* content of the argument (right brain) and Ben is focused on the *logical* content of the argument (left brain).

The last thing Penny needed was the voice of reason. What she really needed was support.

Penny feels immensely frustrated that Ben has not understood and acknowledged her *feelings* and Ben is puzzled as to why his logical explanations have not persuaded Penny that she is wrong.

Here are a couple of key things Penny and Ben would do well to remember next time:

Every conflict has two components – an **emotional component** and a **rational component**.

When a person experiences high emotion in response to a situation or an exchange with another person, the rational, thinking part of their brain will not work unless and until they have dealt with the emotional hijacking of their brain.

It is physically impossible for someone to switch to logical thinking when their Amygdala has created an emotional fight or flight response. What Ben needs to do first is to find a way to calm Penny's emotions and one of the best ways to do this is to *empathise* with her.

Empathy is the ability to imagine yourself in someone else's position and to understand or intuit what that person is *feeling* – to be able to sense their pain or discomfort and respond to it. Yet we are often embarrassed and tend to shy away from emotional and empathic exchanges.

Here's the *key thing* to remember – **acknowledge a person's emotional state with an empathic response**. If you can find the words with which you are most comfortable and can naturally express, 'It sounds like you are feeling very frustrated,' or 'I can see that you are upset by this,' you will be taking the first steps to resolving the situation without a battle taking place.

Penny needs Ben to tune into her emotional wavelength and match the intensity of her feelings: 'What a pig of a time you're having.' She needs to know that he is attempting to understand the point she is trying to make, which might be more about other issues – a tough day at work or problems with childcare – than simply an overflowing rubbish bin. So it is important that Ben reflects or summarises back to Penny what he thinks he is hearing, giving her an opportunity to correct him if he is wrong.

Reflecting back

So how do we know that we have received and understood the message that the speaker intended to convey? And how does the person speaking feel confident that their words have conveyed exactly the right meaning to their listener?

Unless we take the important step of reflecting back to the speaker what we thought we heard and checking that our interpretation is correct, then we have no real way of knowing that we have understood accurately.

We don't need to repeat back exactly what we have heard but to *summarise* the important bits – the essence of what the other person was saying.

Phrases such as:

'You seem to be suggesting…'

'So what I heard was…'

'If I heard you correctly…'

'So what you think is that...'

are all useful ways to reflect your understanding.

Reflecting back reassures the other person that you *have* been listening and that you *have* been taking them seriously. It also gives the speaker the opportunity to correct our understanding of what they have said.

Speaking to someone who gives the impression that they are not listening to you because:

- they are not making eye contact with you

- they are engaged in another activity – such as reading the paper or watching television

- they are thinking about something else

- they are too busy crafting their response

is a lonely and soul destroying activity.

Giving your interpretation

The loop of listening is not complete unless and until we have given the speaker some information about our response to their message. The idea is that we add some *new information* to the picture about how we feel or what we think as a result of what they have said.

Ben also needs to give Penny some feedback as to his own interpretation of her message, this he needs to do in a sensitive or tentative way – 'I may be off track here, but I feel...' 'My present feeling about this is...'

Our interpretation should never be an attack on what has just been said, which will simply provoke a defensive response. It must add some value to the conversation, describing our reaction rather than criticising the speaker or what they have just said.

The rules for good listeners

1. Listen for understanding

    – what important message is the speaker trying to convey?

2. Empathise with the speaker

    – discern and respond to the mood of the speaker.

3. Reflect/playback what you heard

    – summarise or paraphrase.

4. Feedback your interpretation

    – say what you feel and think in response to the speaker's message.

We need to:

- Show that we understood what the person said

- Recognise how they feel about it

- Give some feedback regarding how we feel about the message.

Good listening and conversation is at the heart of every successful relationship and poor listening and conversation is the root of many relationship breakdowns and the basis of most conflicts and disputes.

Listening is a gift

One of the most valuable gifts we can give to others is the gift of listening. To be truly listened to is to receive a precious gift from someone who is saying in effect, 'I am putting you first.'

True listening is a very courageous act because it involves seriously entertaining the ideas, values and perceptions of the other person and putting your own ideas and instinctive responses on hold while you do so.

We cannot find personal intimacy without listening. When we are listening, we are offering the other person the gift of understanding and acceptance (not agreement) – the gift of taking that person seriously.

"When we are listened to, it creates us, makes us unfold and expand. Ideas actually begin to grow within us and come to life. You know how if a person laughs at your jokes you become funnier and funnier, and if he does not, every tiny little joke in you weakens up and dies. Well, that is the principle of it. It makes people happy and free when they are listened to. And if you are a listener, it is the secret of having a good time in society (because everybody around you becomes lively and interesting), of comforting people, of doing them good."

— Strength to Your Sword Arm:
Selected Writings by Brenda Ueland
(From a collection of her essays).
(Copyright 1992 by The Estate of Brenda Ueland.)

In a nutshell

All communication is about creating understanding.

Whether you are the speaker or the listener, the key is to show that you understand the other person and what's important to them.

"Be a good listener. Unlike your mouth, your ears will never get you in trouble."

— Frank Tyger

10: GETTING YOUR PRIORITIES RIGHT

Why it helps to see issues in perspective

> *"To see life from the perspective of intuition is like looking at life from the summit of the mountain, whereas seeing life only from the perspective of intellect is like looking at life from the foot of the mountain."*
>
> — Swami Dhyan Giten

BEDLAM
IN THE BOARDROOM

Christopher is immersed in a claim for unfair dismissal and discrimination against his former employers, a large pharmaceutical company where he worked as a sales manager. As the tribunal hearing approaches, Christopher spends his days in meetings with his lawyers and is reading legal papers until late into the night. He no longer has much time to spend with his family, can't sleep at night and is exhausted.

When he developed Chronic Fatigue two years ago at the age of 48, following a nasty bout of flu (caught from one of the directors who insisted on coming in to work) he believed that he would be looked after and would receive help in readjusting to the pace of life at work. Instead he was made to feel that his illness was 'all in the head' and that he was some sort of malingerer.

To make matters worse Christopher's line manager, Ted, retired from the company at about the same time as he became ill and was replaced by Sam who was young and ambitious and keen to change the way the sales team operated.

It seemed to Christopher that instead of lightening his work load Sam was going out of his way to make the working day longer and more difficult. Sam's departmental reorganisation meant that Christopher had more miles to drive and a more challenging sales team to manage.

One day, desperate to make Sam understand his condition and see the impact the new regime was having on him, Christopher told him that he was experiencing blinding headaches while driving and often felt that he literally couldn't see straight by the end of the day. Sam's immediate reaction was to suspend Christopher from work indefinitely, because he said it was no longer safe for him to perform his duties. So, instead of being understood and cared for, Christopher was made to feel inadequate and, unable to communicate with Sam, his reaction was to resign.

Now Christopher is without a job and does not have much prospect of rejoining the pharmaceutical industry at his age. What he would secretly like to do next is to launch a web business to promote and sell some of the remedies that have helped him to recover from his illness. But at the moment he cannot give up the fight no matter what impact it has on his life and health.

BEDROOM

BOREDOM IN THE

Christopher's daughter, Sophie, is getting married. Sophie and her mother, Sue, have been planning the wedding for months. Sophie met Philippe in Argentina when she was travelling after her degree. Sophie is very excited about the wedding, which is only three months away now, but Sue is desperately worried.

From what Sophie has said Philippe comes from a wealthy land-owning family in Argentina and Sue is keen to put on a good show. The plans are for a marquee in the grounds of a local hotel, but as Sue adds up the cost of it all including the caterers and the band and with Christopher now out of work, she is filled with a rising sense of panic.

To make matters worse Christopher refuses to discuss the wedding plans especially the costs. Sophie is his only daughter and he doesn't want to disappoint her or let her down.

Even worse than his concern about the costs, Christopher is dreading having to make the Father of the Bride speech. What with his illness and now with the job loss and stress of legal proceedings, his confidence has reached rock bottom. He would rather parachute from a plane than have to stand up in front of all the guests and try and impress them and be witty. Sophie is unaware of all of this. She is madly in love with Philippe and all they want is to be together.

The forest or the trees

Why is it that when we encounter a major problem or conflict it's tempting to blow it out of all proportion so that it turns into a major stumbling block and prevents us from moving forwards?

Christopher cannot see any way out of his current situation at work or at home. He is determined to go ahead with his legal action against his employers and with Sophie's wedding. Despite the effect that both are having on his rising stress levels, he can't see any way out. It's like this:

Imagine that you are standing by a giant oak tree. If you look straight ahead of you all you can see is the trunk with its gnarled and knotted bark. If you look above or to the side, you are surrounded by a tangle of branches and a canopy of leaves. Everything appears in a shade of brown or green. You are engulfed by the tree just as you are by the problem or conflict that overshadows your life.

But what if you were to take a few steps back from the tree? Now you can see a few trees, a rocky path and, in the distance, a mountain.

As you walk along the path and begin to climb the mountain you see that the trees are in fact part of a larger woodland area. Climb a little higher and you can see farmland beyond the woods. Higher still and you can see a village and beyond that a distant town… until you reach the top and you have a full 360 degree view.

See the big picture

The problem

Christopher is overwhelmed by the need to prepare for the fight against his former employers and to prove that they are to blame for his current plight.

Christopher is also overwhelmed by the plans for the wedding and his need to show his love and support for Sophie and not to let her down.

The larger reality

What if seeing things from a different perspective helped Christopher to see that family and long-term health are just as important as 'winning' his case?

What if he could also see the situation from the company's perspective and see the possibility that Sam, while ambitious, was not being vindictive, but was simply a poor communicator and listener, unable to understand Christopher's illness and express empathy?

What if Christopher could see that Sophie's relationship with Philippe and her father's health and happiness, is more important to her than a grand wedding and that, secretly, they would much rather have a smaller, quieter celebration.

Would those perspectives help Christopher to see things differently?

Finding the time and the space to take a step back from our problems and to see the 'big picture' can be an important step on the way to resolution.

But how do we begin to do this when we quite literally 'cannot see the wood for the trees'? There are three important steps that we can take:

1. Share the story.

2. Separate the people from the problem.

3. Focus on the future and not the past.

Share the story

The saying goes that 'a problem shared is a problem halved'. So what is it about telling or sharing our story that helps us to gain a different perspective?

The newspapers are full of stories of people who are so incensed by what has happened to them that they want to 'tell the world'. People in the public eye often justify selling their story to the press or writing about events in their memoirs by the need to 'set the record straight' or 'tell the truth'.

Litigants also often relish the opportunity to have their 'day in court'. The desire here is to gain support for their own position and to have the public, or the judge, declare the other person to be totally wrong or out of order.

Often when we tell someone about a situation or person we do so because we want them to join us in judging or critiquing the other person. We want them to confirm what we thought all along, that *we are right*, and *the other party is wrong*.

On the other hand, genuinely sharing your story with a colleague, friend or relative can have an entirely different effect. Choosing someone who is a good listener and having your story reflected back to you as you tell it can help you to gain a wider perspective. This is especially true if your listening friend can help you to challenge all the assumptions that you may have made along the way.

As you *tell* your story you are also *listening to yourself* tell it.

Challenging assumptions and trying to understand what may be driving the other person's view is an important part of storytelling.

The key question here is 'what if?'

What if Sam was not pursuing a personal vendetta against Christopher as he *assumes*, but instead there was some other explanation for his behaviour?

What if Philippe's parents are dreading the big wedding as much as Christopher is?

Sometimes sharing our story can help us come to the realisation that the other people in our conflict or dispute are also vulnerable human beings. Maybe they are trying to sustain their own world view and uphold their values and beliefs, just as we are. And when we can find values and attitudes that we share with each other, at whatever level, then we can truly begin to understand each other and to connect.

Separate the people from the problem

Why is it that some issues are so hard to resolve? Emotions run high, people misunderstand each other and harsh words are exchanged.

The reason is that the problem that needs to be resolved – the employment contract or the family issue – gets tied up and confused with the relationships between the people involved.

Christopher's claim against his employers is overshadowed by his *feelings* about his relationship with Sam. If they were to meet face-to-face he would find it almost impossible not to view Sam as an adversary and to treat anything that he said about the problem as directed against him personally.

Christopher's issues about the wedding similarly are overshadowed by his feelings about his daughter and her fiancé and any comment by Sue or Sophie may be perceived by Christopher as a personal attack against him.

So often when we try to resolve our problems, we are blinded by the WHO in the conversation and the WHAT takes a back seat.

We tend to see our negotiations as a conflict of wills or egos and to conclude that the other person's contrary position on the problem simply demonstrates how little they care about or value their relationship with us.

The first thing to understand is that conflict is not based in reality, but in what goes on in people's heads. The difference is in people's thinking about the problem rather than in the problem itself. So the place to start is with the *other person's reality* to try to see the world from where they stand – quite literally *'put yourself in their shoes'*.

The key is to deal with the people issues separately from the substantive issues. To begin by viewing the other person as a sensitive human being with important values and beliefs and a strong need to protect their own ego. What we must then do is to find ways to communicate clearly our perception of the problem, and then help the other person to clearly communicate theirs.

We must be sure to acknowledge and respect their view (understanding their point of view is not the same as agreeing with it) and take time to explore and correct any misunderstanding. Letting off steam and managing high emotions can be an important part of this process.

Then and only then you can sit side-by-side as problem-solving partners rather than adversaries and face the common task of trying to find a solution to the problem.

Focus on the future and not the past

The focus of most conflicts and disputes is the past.

The people involved often spend much of their time going back over what happened in the past in intricate detail, trying to allocate blame or fault. Most formal grievance and dispute resolution processes are based on exactly this premise.

Christopher is still focused on what his employers have done wrong and how badly they have treated him in the past. Even his concerns about the wedding are focused on how his employers are to blame for his current financial situation and lack of confidence.

However, a new and different perspective can be gained by focusing on the future and a time when the conflict or dispute no longer exists. Christopher could imagine a point – somewhere between one and five years ahead – and describe in detail the circumstances, relationships, feelings etc. In other words, to visualise exactly what life might be like when the conflict or dispute is no longer part of the picture. It can also be helpful to focus on 'best outcomes' and 'worst outcomes' and to work out exactly what is important in those scenarios.

Christopher might say that what he would like most for the future is to be running his own successful web business and to have a more balanced and less stressful life (his best outcome). He might also say that there is the possibility that he is so knocked back by what has happened and the subsequent court case that he will not be able to regain his health or confidence and make a fresh start (his worst outcome).

Once these visions of the future are articulated and made real, it is possible to look at what is required and plan the steps necessary to achieve the best outcome rather than make the worst outcome a reality.

In a nutshell

Seeing the 'big picture' and focusing on what matters most is a great way to get issues in perspective when you begin the search for solutions.

"Every now and then go away and have a little relaxation. To remain constantly at work will diminish your judgment. Go some distance away, because work will be in perspective and a lack of harmony is more readily seen."

— **Leonardo da Vinci**

11: ANOTHER PARTY?

Can someone else bring a new dimension?

> *"The wise man doesn't give the right answers, he poses the right questions."*
>
> — Claude Levi-Strauss

BEDLAM

IN THE BOARDROOM

Four business partners, Jim, Louise, Clive and David, sit outside court and wait for the judge to arrive, they have reached the end of the road. They will ask the court to dissolve the partnership and determine the amount each partner will receive, the business will be wound up and they will go their separate ways.

Each partner has his own legal team to represent him, two partners are no longer speaking and one is receiving medical treatment and counselling for stress and depression as a result of the business break up. Each will fight the other to gain the settlement they feel is right under the terms of the partnership agreement.

BEDROOM

BOREDOM IN THE

Jim has had enough of work – his wife, Sarah, has been trying to persuade him that it's time he retired so that they can travel as they had always planned. He feels guilty that he is still working, but also feels that he has an obligation to the business and feels that it's his 'baby'.

David doesn't need any more stress, but he doesn't feel able to share his domestic problems. His daughter has been receiving treatment for drug and alcohol abuse and he has been spending time and money trying to help her. His attention to the business has taken second place to his daughter.

A different point of view

Four business partners, Jim, Louise, Clive and David, smile and shake hands.

After ten hours in mediation a totally different picture has emerged from this dispute.

During the mediation the mediator has discovered:

- David has run up huge expense accounts, offended clients, been sharp and abusive in meetings and has been siphoning money from one of the business accounts causing the business to spiral downward.

- Jim has refused to acknowledge the impact of David's behaviour, they are old school chums and go back a long way.

- David's daughter's situation has been brought out into the open.

- Jim's wish to retire has been made clear.

- Clive and Louise expressed that they want to try and rescue the business.

- David wants to work for the charity that helped his daughter.

The mediator has helped the partners to explore the breakdown of their business relationship, helped them to understand what each wants as an outcome now and helped them formulate an agreement to reach that outcome that all have now signed.

Clive and Louise have agreed to continue the business with a new vision and purpose and with the specific aim of supporting a local charity that provides rehabilitation for troubled teenagers. David will work for the charity and receive an agreed payment for his share in the business. Jim will retire, but continue to support Clive and Louise as a consultant.

The benefits

What difference does it make to bring in a third party to help you to resolve your dispute? What has a mediator achieved that Jim, Louise, Clive and David could not do on their own?

Face-to-face negotiation is fraught with problems. The two main concerns that prevent us from dealing directly with people with whom we have a conflict or dispute are:

- *Lack of trust*: we are not sure that we can trust each other enough to be open and honest

- *Fear of emotions*: we are not sure that we can handle our own and others' emotional reactions.

David was so embarrassed about his daughter's drug and alcohol problems that he hid the whole experience from his partners and he is still not certain of their reactions. Working with a mediator has helped him to talk about some of the very real issues that are behind the partnership breakdown; discover his own and others' feelings and emotions, and work out ways to communicate and negotiate in a more effective way.

Inviting a person who has no involvement in the dispute to work with us can help because we can share information, thoughts, feelings and ideas with them in confidence. We can work with the third party on identifying needs, interests and concerns, work out what's important and what our real priorities are, discuss options and ideas for resolution and test out assumptions, all without compromising our own position, at least until we are confident that everyone concerned is working in good faith towards a resolution.

Who can help?

Can anyone act as a trusted third party to help resolve a dispute? In theory, the answer is 'yes', friends, neighbours and relatives can, and do, act as unofficial and untrained mediators all the time. Mothers mediate between fighting children, relatives get embroiled in matrimonial strife, passers-by attempt to placate warring motorists. But the reality is that using a trained mediator is a safer option, especially where the issues are important and where continuity of the conflict or dispute could be costly and/or painful.

So finding a trained or professional mediator is a good idea, but what are you looking for?

The best mediators have a natural ability to gain trust and rapport, they understand the dynamics of dispute, how and why warring parties behave as they do, how to listen and how to ask effective questions to uncover hidden interests and agendas. They are also skilled in managing strong emotions and diverse personalities and perspectives.

The magic of mediation

A mediator's key role is to be neutral with no vested interest whatsoever in whether an outcome to the dispute is reached and what it might look like. A good mediator is merely a facilitator, helping others to communicate and negotiate effectively.

The expertly *skilled* mediator will help the people involved to form a deeper understanding of the dispute and of the underlying motives and behaviours of all concerned. Sometimes acting as a confidant to each party separately, he or she can help them to transform their attitude towards the dispute, to reach a deep level of honesty and empathy and to explore different options as to how it might be resolved and, in the end, transcended.

The magic of mediation occurs when those involved finally come to see the vulnerable human beings behind the demon's masks they had perceived and are able to move beyond the dispute itself by listening, learning and discovering about themselves as well as each other.

By involving a mediator, Jim, Louise, Clive and David have discovered a different reality and understood the misperceptions and miscommunications of the past. They are now able to work towards a different but more creative future than the legal action would have offered them.

What makes it work?

What would it take for you to entrust a third party with your deepest thoughts and feelings about a critical issue? What is it that makes the relationship with a neutral third party different from any other?

At its best, mediation creates a unique relationship and dynamic for communication between the mediator and individuals involved. It does so partly as a result of the skill of the mediator and partly as a result of various ground-rules, which, in a formal mediation, will be written into a mediation agreement and signed by the all those attending the meeting or meetings.

The most important ground rule is *confidentiality*. For a mediator to fully understand what is really driving a person's position or stand on an issue it is necessary for the mediator to ask some fairly sensitive and penetrating questions. The certainty that this information will be held in complete and utter confidence and will absolutely not be shared with anyone else, either inside or outside the mediation, unless and until permission is given, is the key to success.

As the mediator meets with each person involved he or she is gradually able to add new pieces to the jigsaw puzzle and to see a different picture emerge. Then, when it becomes clearer which information it would be helpful to share to move closer to finding a solution, permission can be sought.

For example, Jim had not shared with any of his partners his secret wish to retire from the business and found it quite liberating to share this thought with the mediator. As it became clear that each partner had some confidential information never before revealed, the mediator was able to ask for permission to share whatever was necessary to help the partners see the true picture and find a new way forward.

Other factors that are critical to the success of mediation are that everyone is there willingly and voluntarily and that those attending, especially in a business context, have the power or authority to make any decisions regarding outcomes or solutions. It is also important that the mediator makes it clear that he or she will not pass any judgment or try to force his or her own ideas on those present.

When to get someone involved

Mediators are usually called upon to help much too late in the day. Typically, as with Jim, Louise, Clive and David, conflict has become dispute, communications have reached deadlock and lawyers are often engaged.

The best time for a mediator to become involved is when direct, face-to-face communication between those involved is no longer possible, where mistrust and suspicion are manifest and where damage and costs, both human and financial, are beginning to escalate.

Whenever face-to-face communication has become difficult or impossible and trust has broken down it is important to act as swiftly as possible. Unfortunately, it is often the case that the people involved are in denial and, therefore, not aware of the unfolding drama and the consequences if they do not act soon.

Alternatively, they are not aware that engaging a third party is a valid alternative to hiring a lawyer and it is rare for people to have in place a plan for dealing with such circumstances.

In a nutshell

There are huge benefits to bringing in a third party to help you resolve your dispute.

The 'Tao' of the Third Party

Go to the people
Live with them
Learn from them
Start with what they know
Build with what they have

And with the best third party
When the work is done
The task completed
The people will say 'We did this ourselves'

— Adapted from a poem by Lao Tsu, China 700BC

12: PLANNING FOR CONFLICT

How to plan for conflict and dispute at work and at home

> "The problem is not that there are problems. The problem is expecting otherwise and thinking that having problems is a problem."
>
> — Theodore Rubin

BEDLAM
IN THE BOARDROOM

The board of the Association of Professional Chefs is in disarray. They cannot agree whether they should accept Stanley's application for membership or not. They are arguing as to whether he has demonstrated his cooking skills to the satisfaction of all the members of the Board.

The trouble is that each of the board members seems to be applying their own very different standards to Stanley's application. Deborah, who has known Stanley for some time on a personal level, believes very strongly that Stanley should cook and serve a Cordon Bleu style meal to a group of diners, including at least one member of the board. Roger disagrees on the basis that Stanley has recently taken part in a TV Master Chef series and thus confirmed his credentials.

The discussions among the board members are going round in circles and they are getting increasingly angry and frustrated with each other. Roger has finally blown his top and offered his resignation to the board on a point of principle. He feels that it is hardly Stanley's fault that the board has not got its act together and been able to clarify the entry criteria and standards. Having delivered his ultimatum he sets off for home with a heavy heart.

BEDROOM

BOREDOM IN THE

Roger arrives home from work exhausted and surveys the scene. Alex, his son, is refusing to do his homework and is slumped in front of the TV. Julie, Roger's wife, has suggested that he ought to make a start and that the work will only start to pile up if he leaves it until tomorrow, but Alex just grunts at her and carries on staring at the hypnotic screen.

Roger has had a long day confronting the issue of Stanley's application and matters of principle and discipline and cannot bear to see this slack attitude. Roger storms into the living room and turns off the TV which leads to a shouting match with Alex and ends in Alex leaving the house (presumably to continue watching the TV at his friend Jack's house).

Roger accuses Julie of letting Alex get away with too much and not supporting his efforts to provide his son with a good education (which he himself did not have). Julie interprets this as an attack on her parenting skills and feels that Roger does not have to deal with Alex on a day-to-day basis and juggle all the chores that she has to. She feels the school regime is too tough and that Alex deserves some time to relax.

Roger and Julie eat their evening meal in silence and wait for Alex to creep back from Jack's house – which he does around midnight.

Firefighting

How do we discover the fact that someone is unhappy or dissatisfied – whether as a partner, customer, supplier or employee? How do we raise issues that we have with others?

Sometimes we let things fester. We delay doing or saying anything about the situation often in the hope that it will go away or, frequently, because we do not know what do next. Unsure of how to progress our complaint or concern, or uncertain what steps should be taken to create a good rather than a bad outcome; we take the safe option and choose not to *rock the boat*.

> *Roger's dissatisfaction with his fellow board members has been brewing for some time with several disagreements arising during the last few months, including the current issue regarding the application process and criteria for new members. But Roger has not said anything because he feared the outcome and that without a clear agreement or policy on managing disagreements he would simply be side-lined by his fellow board members and his comments ignored. In the end this has been a disastrous policy as it has meant that Roger has now reached breaking point and offered to resign. The opportunity to deal with issues at an earlier stage has been missed.*

Systems

Imagine a town or city without a water and drainage system. With no means to manage an excess or a lack of water the value of the resource is lost and, instead, it becomes a risk or a threat. There is no way to prevent flooding or drought.

We manage an over-supply of water by anticipating rainfall and floods and by creating *systems* that capture and manage the flow of water –

water butts, drains, aqueducts and reservoirs. This way, we can use water to our advantage and prevent it getting out of control and causing damage and destruction.

The same rules apply to conflict and disagreement. If we allow it to grow and to fester for too long it will be much harder to manage and more likely to cause *damage and loss*. If, on the other hand, we can find ways for it to be brought to the surface, acknowledged and dealt with then we create the potential to *add value* by finding solutions and repairing relationships.

When people are faced with conflict and they don't know what to do next they often spend too much money, time and emotional energy trying to resolve their problems.

The idea behind a system for managing issues or conflicts is that the individuals involved should be able to choose from a range of options in terms of methods for trying to reach a resolution and that they should always start with the simplest and most cost effective.

Options for resolution

> *For a long time now Roger has avoided dealing with the issue of Alex and his homework. He has chosen not to mention the problem to Julie in the evenings when they are both tired after a long day at work. Except for this evening when all his pent up frustration came tumbling out!*

One option for dealing with issues is avoidance. Sometimes this is the right choice if it allows the parties to cool-off so that they are less likely to react out of anger. Occasionally, an issue will resolve itself, but it is much more likely that avoidance, especially in the long term, will lead to festering emotions and an eventual escalation of hostilities.

> Roger's co-director Deborah has adopted a different approach to boardroom disagreements. She has had secret chats and meetings and schemed and connived with other board members to win them over to her way of thinking and side-line those who do not agree (including Roger). There is of course no formal record of these meetings.

An alternative course of action for some people when they do not feel their concerns are being acknowledged is the use of *power*. This may take the form of physical violence or attack or sabotage and behind-the-scenes manoeuvring. Strikes are a typical example of the use of power in an attempt to *force* the other party to see your point of view.

> Roger feels that he has effectively been forced out of his job by the others, and is now considering bringing a claim for constructive dismissal. As communication with his fellow directors has now broken down completely, this is the only way he can think of to force them to take notice of him and his point of view.

Referring a problem to a *higher authority* to decide who is right and who is wrong is often costly is terms of ongoing relationships, legal fees and time. Sometimes however, it is the only option left to help the parties resolve an issue.

What if Roger and Deborah's organisation were to adopt a deliberate policy on dispute resolution and conflict management? What if the organisation were then able to create an overt culture of *collaboration* and very transparent processes that make it clear how disagreements and conflicts should be dealt with?

Roger and Deborah would then know that the first option they should consider would be a face-to-face meeting between the directors involved in the disagreement. All the directors would have received training in negotiation and conflict management skills. If this first attempt failed, they might then call in a neutral third party to help. Only as a last resort, would the issue be escalated to a higher authority. Formal grievances and costly litigation would be very rarely used and only after all other options have been tried and exhausted.

Grand design

Any system, if it is to work and be used by people, has to be carefully and well designed. Most conflicts and disputes, whether at work or at home, are managed on an ad hoc basis using only whatever responses are available *in the heat of the moment*.

There is often no time for the people involved to stop and take a view:

- What is my best option for resolving this well?

- Is this an issue that keeps causing problems?

- Do I need help and support or can I manage this alone?

Without agreement as to the best way forward, each party will do the best they can with whatever skills and tools they have to hand and, if that fails, the conflict will *escalate* and those involved become increasingly hostile and adversarial.

But, what if there was a system, a way of 'doing things around here' that provided an agreed framework or steps towards resolution. At its simplest, in a family setting, like the one between Julie and Roger over Alex's homework, this could be an agreement between parents that, where one had made a decision in the absence of the other about an important issue, they would not openly criticise the other in front of the child until they had an opportunity to hear the whole story.

In an organisation, the steps or stages of conflict resolution would have to be set out in a more formal way so that they could be easily referred to by everyone. Ideally, all the people who might use the system should be involved in some way or have some say in its design. If this had been the case perhaps Roger and Deborah would not have arrived at this uncomfortable, and potentially expensive, ending to their business relationship.

The chosen design should present a *preferred path* to resolution starting at the simplest level with the parties themselves and giving clear guidelines about when and how to escalate the matter to the next level.

A basic design for a Conflict Management System might look as follows:

Level 1: Direct negotiation – the people involved are usually in the best position to attempt to resolve an issue provided that they have:

- Acknowledged the problem

- Not started the adversarial 'blame game'

- The skills and

- Are prepared to devote the necessary time to do so.

Level 2: Assisted negotiation – involving an independent third party who is not, in any way, involved in the issues between the parties is often the next best step. In an organisational setting this might be a trained mediator or facilitator, but in a family setting may be a trusted friend, acquaintance or family member.

Level 3: Formal resolution – if steps 1 and 2 fail to provide a satisfactory resolution then the issue may (if appropriate) be referred to a higher authority – a tribunal or a court or to a more senior person who can make a decision for those involved.

Any group of people or organisation, whether it is a business, hospital, school or religious organisation, can begin with this basic design and agree the details that are needed to make it work such as:

- WHO instigates each step

- HOW do they do it

- By WHEN do things have to happen

- WHO needs to be involved

- WHEN is it OK to move on to the next step.

It is always challenging to acknowledge and plan for the possibility of conflicts and disputes early on in a business or in family relationships when no problems exist and none seem possible. Yet, we can see that conflicts can prove valuable if issues are flagged up at an early stage when there is still an opportunity to save and even rescue relationships. In this situation we may find the work of planning ahead and designing a system, however simple, may be worth the time and effort.

In a nutshell

Having an agreed system or plan for handling conflicts can help us to manage them more easily and at a much earlier stage, and so avoid the problems and costs of escalation.

"Instead of suppressing conflicts, specific channels could be created to make this conflict explicit, and specific methods could be set up by which the conflict is resolved."

— Albert Low

13: CELEBRATING DIFFERENCE

Why we should welcome conflict as a positive

and not a negative force

> "What people often mean by getting rid of conflict is getting rid of diversity, and it is of utmost importance that these should not be considered the same. We may wish to abolish conflict, but we cannot get rid of diversity... Fear of difference is fear of life itself."
>
> — Mary Parker Follett

BEDLAM
IN THE BOARDROOM

Colin and Jilly, co-directors of a children's charity, have fallen out and are no longer speaking. Colin believes that the telephone answering system that Jilly was responsible for installing a short while ago, is impersonal and that they will lose the goodwill of people calling the charity who find themselves unable to speak to a human being.

Jilly is incensed and sees Colin's criticism as a personal attack on her decision-making capability. She was only trying to use charity funds wisely and avoid the cost of having to hire a full-time receptionist.

Jilly is now having lunch with fellow director, Sandra, and is letting off steam about Colin's behaviour. She confides to Sandra that she often feels that Colin does not listen to or respect her ideas, which makes her feel small and insignificant.

Sandra knows that Colin would be horrified at the idea that he belittles Jilly and feels certain that he does not have any idea of the impact he is having. She suggests that the three of them arrange an informal meeting to try and sort things out.

Sandra is very clever at facilitating this meeting and helps her friends and fellow directors to talk openly and honestly about their working relationship and how they communicate with one another.

Shy at first, Jilly confides that both as a child and young woman she was 'put down' by her father who constantly remarked 'Jilly is silly' and 'You cannot expect anyone to take that idea seriously, Jilly?' As a result, Jilly suffers from a chronic lack of confidence and is often much more defensive at work than she needs to be.

Colin is very sad to learn of Jilly's childhood experiences, especially as the charity they both work for aims to help children. He acknowledges that he is not the best listener and does not pay much attention to what his colleagues are thinking or feeling. The meeting is a huge learning experience for both Colin and Jilly (and for Sandra too) and they end up agreeing some ideas for better communications for all the staff at the charity.

BOREDOM IN THE BEDROOM

Stunned by his lack of self-knowledge and awareness of how his colleagues perceive him, Colin worries that perhaps he is creating a similar situation at home.

One evening he plucks up the courage to discuss his fears with his wife, Karen. They have a long discussion about many things including their different approaches to spending time together and prioritising work and home life. As a result they agree to cut down on working and spending time at the computer in the evenings and at weekends and to take it in turns to arrange a special outing once a month where they will enjoy each other's company and office talk will be banned!

Threat or opportunity?

Why do we see conflict as a threat – as something to be avoided, denied or ignored? Is ignoring or denying its existence a valid option?

Conflict is everywhere – at home and at work, and in society at large between business partners, spouses, parents and children, religions and countries. At its simplest it is an expression of unmet expectations, when what we get does not match what we *thought* we would get.

Unless we have learnt a better way, we react to the unexpected with fear and pain and our actions and responses are unconscious, based more on instinct and ways we have developed from past experiences than on conscious decisions or using learned skills.

Jilly's reaction to Colin is based on the pain and humiliation she experienced as a child in response to her father and her fear of being belittled as an adult in the workplace. Her reaction is based on the 'fight or flight' instinct and her defensive behaviour is the only way she knows to win through.

> "In essence we remain prehistoric in our approach to conflict. In emotional terms we have not developed as fast as the world around us – this in itself is a conflict."
>
> — Gerry Spence
> author of **How to Argue and Win Every Time**

We cannot ignore conflict in the hope that it will go away or assume that we can fight to defend our position. The better option is to change our attitude to conflict.

What do we really want?

Why do we want to win when we are in conflict with others? What is it that we fear and what is it that we hope for?

Sometimes we want to win the moral high ground, to prove that we are right and the other party is wrong. Sometimes we want them to give us something or to do something. Often we haven't a clue what we want – we simply want to win!

Supposing we win, what do we get then? The power and the satisfaction of being right – the smugness and self-righteousness of being able to think or to say, 'I told you so,' and all the better if we can display our power and might to others too.

In essence, every conflict begins inside us. We want to win and be proved right because we want to feel OK about ourselves. If someone takes away our power and control over our circumstances or the way we see the world or our self-image then we react out of fear and in anger. If we are made to feel diminished in some way then we must fight to regain our sense of dignity and control – our self-esteem.

Our ultimate fear is that we are unlovable and unloved.

Both Jilly and Colin want to feel comfortable and confident with whom they are, both in the workplace and at home. They need to know that they fit in and are accepted.

In all our exchanges, we seek to find the true meaning of our existence. The questions we ask are 'Who am I?' and 'Where do I belong?' and we yearn to know 'Do I matter?' and 'Am I heard?'

Changing our approach

What if we could believe that all conflict exists for a reason?

If we never experienced or expressed our dissatisfaction or disappointment with others or with the way things work, there would be no motivation or catalyst for change.

If we simply accepted that *this is the way things are around here* we would never learn from our mistakes or explore the possibilities for an alternative way.

But, if instead of regarding conflict as a personal attack, which threatens our very being, we could accept it as *feedback* about circumstances or behaviour delivered without judgment or malice, then rather than turning inward and seeking to defend ourselves we could turn outward and look at the options for change.

> "*Every conflict we face in life is rich with positive and negative potential. It can be a source of inspiration, enlightenment, learning, transformation, and growth – or rage, fear, shame, entrapment, and resistance. The choice is not up to our opponents, but to us, and our willingness to face and work through them.*"
>
> **— Kenneth Cloke and Joan Goldsmith**

It is what we do with conflict that makes a difference – our attitude or approach that can turn it from a negative situation into a positive opportunity.

The first thing that we need to do, and we have to learn to do it, is switch off our instinctive adversarial response. We can do this firstly by telling ourselves: '*This is not personal*' – but we have to believe it and act on that belief. Secondly, we must ask ourselves two questions: '*Why is this happening now?*' and '*What might I learn from this?*'

Once we understand that failures or conflicts are not negative, simply learning experiences that offer the opportunity for growth and change, then we can accept and even welcome the knowledge that sometimes we get it wrong and that getting it wrong could be the best thing that ever happened to us.

If Jilly and Colin had not been given the opportunity to examine their attitudes and behaviour in a deep and honest way, they would not have learnt what was blocking their relationships with each other and also with family and friends. They would not have been able to benefit from that knowledge.

Barriers to change

All of this is easy in theory, so what is that prevents us from accepting and welcoming conflict as we go about our everyday lives?

Apart from our instinctive, inbuilt responses to perceived threat, we are also conditioned by a lifetime of learned responses. Everything that we have learned and experienced on our journey through life so far is etched in our psyche.

The tendency to fight is so deeply ingrained in our thoughts and feelings because we have witnessed so many others approach conflict in this way. If our parents have fought, our teachers been self-righteous and defensive, our work colleagues gossiped behind our backs and we have seen countless other mishandled conflicts and wars reported in the media, then we are already programmed to adopt the wrong approach.

Step by step we need to learn new skills and to practise a new approach.

To truly change our attitude and approach to conflict we need to find someone to teach and guide us; someone who models these new behaviours and who can offer both encouragement and wisdom. We may need to go on a course or to find someone who can coach or mentor us. And then what we need is commitment, persistence and above all practice!

Four stages of learning

Once we understand our own barriers to change and have understood what skills and tools we can adopt to change our approach to conflict, the next step is to get really good at using them.

Current knowledge of how our brains work teaches us that, in order to get really good at something, we have to be able to bypass conscious thought and act or behave unconsciously.

Similar to learning to ride a bike or drive a car, the transformation is broken down into four stages:

1. Unconscious incompetence – this is when we are unaware that we are not very good.

2. Conscious incompetence – we become aware of our own shortcomings and of what it would be like to be good, yet when we compare ourselves with others we can sense that we still have a long way to go.

3. Conscious competence – now we have acquired a level of skill, but we have to think consciously to perform well.

4. Unconscious competence – practising the skill feels natural and requires little or no conscious thought.

Both good and bad habits are learned by this method and so the only way to change our attitude and behaviour during conflict situations is to practise. If you really do want to change you'll need to learn a new and better way and then to repeat it over and over again until the subconscious is reprogrammed.

Dare to be different

What is the greatest danger that we face in managing conflict? Often it is not the conflict itself but our unwillingness to find out what it is really about.

One of our greatest fears is of difference and of people who are different to us in some way.

We experience life according to our own world view – in other words, our beliefs, values, experiences etc. – and we are afraid of people who see things differently. The more fragile our own self-concept or self-esteem, the more threatened we are by any suggestion that we are wrong because this seems to threaten the very foundations of our being.

Faced with conflict, our natural tendency is to persuade or to force the other to change – to change their mind, to change their attitude, to change their behaviour.

But stop for a minute and think – what if we were all the same? What if we all shared the same religious and political views, liked the same music and sports, and preferred the same work? We can only exist, work and trade together as human beings precisely because we are all different – because one person likes to fish and the other likes to eat fish.

Without difference we would live in a zero-sum world without any possibility for adding value or growth.

Conflict is a gift specifically because it highlights the differences between us. If we can dare to be different then we can begin to look for the value rather than for the threat in that difference.

To accept the gift of conflict, we must dare to be different and to look beyond our differences to understand each human being as a unique individual and to embrace the possibilities presented to us.

We must be:

- Willing to seek to understand each other

- Ready to change ourselves

- Prepared to collaborate to find value.

In a nutshell

In the end, conflicts are resolved by those people who can acknowledge the humanity and celebrate the differences of their opponents.

"Don't be afraid of opposition. Remember, a kite rises against, not with, the wind."
— Hamilton Mabie

14: WALKING THE TALK

Putting it all into action

> "I challenge you to make your life a masterpiece.
> I challenge you to join the ranks of those people who live
> what they teach, who walk their talk."
>
> — Anthony Robbins

Common sense and common practice

You may think that this book is simply full of common sense! As you read or flick your way through it you will probably say to yourself, 'But I already know that!' This is true of most of the business and personal development books that we read, but the truth is that just because something is common sense does NOT mean that it is common practice. How many of us truly apply all of the tips and tools that we learn about even though we know that they could make a significant difference to our life?

Why don't we do it? Because in our ultra busy, information packed 21st century lives we are bombarded with information and we do not know HOW to do it or WHERE to start.

So here is a step-by-step guide to help you to put conflict management to work in your business and home and achieve startling results.

We will review the **key principles** from each chapter and what you can do to put them into practice.

1: Know the cost of not acting

Conflict affects us all

If we have children or parents or partners or neighbours or colleagues – if we have any relationships at all, we are bound to run into conflict, so we might as well prepare ourselves for it and equip ourselves to cope with it when it happens.

Add it up

How much might an ongoing conflict or dispute be costing you?

Advice	The cost of any professional or other advice you have sought	
Productivity	Time spent dealing with this and productivity lost as a result	
Relationships	Important relationships damaged as a result	
Health	Possible impact on health – short- and long-term	

Warning signs

Is this you?

1. Will *deny danger* or potential disruption if it is inconvenient.

2. *Disbelief prevails over reality* – even when there are warning signs, you will dismiss a threat if it has never happened before.

3. Even when you know that problems might occur, you *seldom make plans* for dealing with them until they do!

Catch it early

You have a **window of opportunity** from the moment that you or others begin to feel unhappy about the way another or others are behaving or the way in which a situation is unfolding.

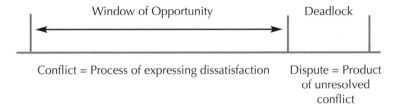

Window of Opportunity · Deadlock

Conflict = Process of expressing dissatisfaction · Dispute = Product of unresolved conflict

Fig 14.1

Know WHO and WHAT matter most

WHO matters most to you in your business and personal life? **WHY?**	
WHAT matters most to that person or those people in terms of your relationship and or business dealings with them? **WHY?**	
WHAT matters most to you? **WHY?**	
Have you taken any steps to communicate this information to each other?	

Remember the journey from conflict to resolution requires **foresight** and **preparation**.

2: Create a safe way to address issues and concerns

Good and bad points in a relationship are hidden behind a mask or veneer of sociability. Creating a safe way to address issues and concerns is the key to constructive resolution and deeper relationships.

Do you know what the people who matter most to you, in business or at home, really think of you?

On what level do you communicate with the people that matter most to you?

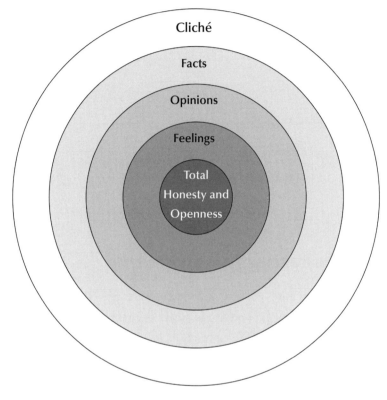

Fig 14.2 [1]

How do you *show* that you are unhappy with someone or something?

How do they *show* you?

- Silence – not speaking to one another

- Talking behind someone's back – gossip and innuendo

- Withholding information

- Sabotage

- Fighting – verbal or physical.

What were you *expecting* that has not happened or been said?

What was the other (or others) *expecting* of you?

I was expecting:

....

They may have been expecting:

....

3:   Understand why you see things differently

We interpret everything we see, hear or experience according to our pre-existing view of the world and our instinctive reaction to difference and conflict is to defend our ideas and beliefs. Being prepared to learn about, understand and acknowledge each other's perspective is the key to good relationships and to resolving conflict.

The world as you see it, is simply the world as *you* see it.

All your experiences to date have created the knowledge, attitudes, values, beliefs and convictions that form *your individual view of the world*.

Everything that you see, hear or experience is interpreted according to *your pre-existing view of the world*, the frame within which you are already operating.

Your instinctive reaction may be to *defend your views* and to *reassert your opinions* in the belief that you can persuade or, if necessary, force others to change their mind.

My interpretation	What's most important to	I feel strongly about this
The way I see the situation is…	me is…	because…
Their interpretation	What's most important to	They feel strongly about
The way they see the situation is...	them is...	this because...

The information that is missing is *how* and *why* **you** and **they** see things **differently** and what is most important to you both about those views and beliefs.

4: Know how you and others may react in a crisis

* Our instinctive reaction to conflict is to see it as a threat and to fight, flee, freeze or appease.

* Once we understand this we can take time to ask ourselves questions about the situation and use our whole brain to consciously decide what the best response would be.

Instinctive responses

The primitive part of the brain called the Amygdala reacts to the **perception** of threat (physical or social). The Amygdala acts much faster than the logical, thinking part of the brain and the only answers it provides us with are:

* Fight
* Flee
* Freeze
* Appease.

Any conflict, that is anything that threatens our needs and interests – our values, attitudes and beliefs, is reacted to as if it were an immediate threat to our survival.

How do you react?

What is your preferred response?

Think back to the last time that you were in a situation where your instinctive reaction to conflict snapped into play. What did you do?

- Did you fight – use physical or verbal aggression?

- Did you flee – storm off or walk away from the situation?

- Did you freeze – react as though nothing had happened?

- Did you appease – try to stop the conflict by offering concessions?

Are there other factors involved?

Think whether there may be other factors that explain your own or other's reaction to the current situation. Examples include:

- A past experience

- A build up of stress

- Low blood sugar

- Lack of sleep.

Engage the *whole* brain

It is possible to teach ourselves to have the whole brain working in situations of threat or conflict. We have to accept that what we first experience is instinctive and not reasoned.

Then we have to ask ourselves three questions:

1. What's really happening here – is this a real emergency?

2. What are some alternative realities to my original perception?

3. Who else matters – what matters to them?

5:   Discover needs, interests, fears and concerns

Discovering each person's needs, interests, fears and concerns is more important than fighting to disprove their position on an issue. People need to be supported to face their fears and look at the world and the problem from a different perspective.

Winning is not always about attaining or acquiring what we want, but about discovering what it is that we really need.

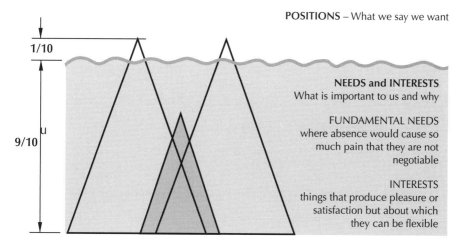

Fig 14.3

The 'Iceberg' Model
like an iceberg 9/10 of important information is hidden [2]

Other people have needs and interests, fears and concerns that are every bit as important as our own and finding ways to acknowledge and meet them is far **more important** than 'winning'.

[2] Adapted from a model by Andrew Acland

Needs	Interests	Fears & Concerns
What I need *I cannot walk away from this unless I achieve the following...*	What I would like *The following are also important to me...*	What worries me most *I am concerned/afraid that...*
What they need *They cannot walk away from this unless they achieve the following...*	What they would like *The following are also important to them...*	What worries them most *They are concerned/afraid that...*

Needs and interests may be driven by:

Fact

What has actually happened and what people expect to happen next.

Behaviour

How people have treated each other in the past and how they intend to treat them in the future.

Beliefs and Values

People's beliefs, whether based on religion, ideology or personal values. These form the basis for their judgment about what is important; good or bad.

People often find it difficult to talk about their beliefs and values and often fear that others will be suspicious or intolerant of them.

Identity

Most important to resolving any kind of dispute is people's sense of self, including their sense of what is vital to them in terms of physical and psychological survival.

6: Learn how your brain is wired

- Each of us falls somewhere on a spectrum between extreme male and extreme female brain.

- Our values, attitudes and behaviour are affected by our biologically determined brain sex.

- We need to both acknowledge and appreciate these differences in our dealings with one another at work and at home.

Male v. female brains

Discovering whether you (and others) are more right or left brained can help you to understand preferences when viewing situations of conflict.

People whose brains are wired mainly for feminine thinking are more likely to make decisions and deal with problems based on **intuition or gut feeling** and are more likely to be creative and insightful (right brain traits). People whose brains are wired mainly for masculine thinking are likely to make decisions and deal with problems using **statistical data, logic and analysis** with their emotions hardly influencing them at all (left brain traits).

Various tests exist to help you determine your own brain sex. Go to http://www.bbc.co.uk/science/humanbody/sex/add_user.shtml on the BBC website or you can measure your fingers.

How to measure your fingers

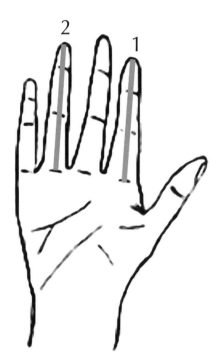

Fig 14.4 [3]

Straighten your fingers and look at the palm of your hand.

At the base of your index and ring finger there are creases. Your index finger is likely to have one crease, the ring finger a band of creases.

Select the crease closest to the palm and choose a point on the crease midway across the base of the finger.

Mark it with a pen.

Measure from the mark to the tip of the finger.

This measurement is important because the base of the ring finger is lower on the hand than the base of the index finger.

Do this for both right and left hands.

Now divide the length of the index finger by the length of the ring finger.

Now you have a ratio. If it is less than one, the ring finger is longer, if the ratio is greater than one; your index finger is longer.

7: Love yourself and your neighbour

- Love and fear are at the heart of most conflicts

- Learn to give love, respect, care and attention to others even when you are in disagreement.

Two principle states of mind

Love and fear are the two principle states of mind.

Anger, jealousy, worry and depression are all expressions of fear.

What we are usually most afraid of is that other people do not love and respect us enough.

[3] *The Finger Book* by John Manning

Three senses of self

Self-esteem – Self-esteem is your emotional opinion of yourself – how you feel about yourself as a person.

Self-confidence – People with strong self-confidence know they can count on themselves more than they can count on anyone else.

Self-concept – Self-concept refers to your idea about who or what you are.

In order to be happy, to have good relationships and be psychologically balanced, we need to feel good about ourselves. We literally need to love ourselves.

Our sense of self determines whether we interpret a disagreement with a colleague as a deliberate attempt to undermine us or a misunderstanding to be resolved.

Trust and respect

The key principle to remember is that every human's moment-to-moment test for trust and respect is

- *Do I matter?* and

- *Am I heard?*

If, in our communications with others, we feel that our ***needs, interests, fears and concerns*** have been acknowledged and understood then we will sense that we *do* matter and that we *have* been heard. When this happens we are more likely to co-operate with others in resolving any problem or conflict.

If, on the other hand, we feel that our ***needs, interests, fears and concerns*** *have not* been acknowledged and understood, we will sense that we *do not matter* and that we are *not heard*. When this happens we may sabotage any attempts to resolve any problem or conflict.

Reach out

People in conflict are longing for a sign that they are loved and respected. If we can show them that as fellow humans they matter and we care then we have taken the first step.

8: Look for an outcome where both can 'win'

Winning should be about getting what we need at the same time as helping others to get what they need.

Wanting to win

We want to win because we are programmed to survive.

The fight or flight response primes us to react instinctively to immediate threats. It is designed to protect us from danger and death and creates both alertness and fear that prompt us to act in self-preservation.

Motivation

The brain chemical dopamine plays a critical role in keeping us motivated when the going gets tough.

Some people get addicted to the 'dopamine buzz' when risk results in reward and seek to repeat the feeling of winning.

Anti-climax

The journey to success is often more rewarding than the destination.

People often report feeling depressed when they finally 'win' unless they had some higher purpose or nobler goal.

High synergy

Winning should be about empowering rather than overpowering others.

Wanting and needing to have things work out well for everyone involved.

That means looking for an outcome that meets our own and other's needs and interests.

My needs and interests	Possible options	Their needs and interests

9: Speak and listen to create understanding

- All communication is about creating understanding.

- Whether you are the speaker or the listener, the key is to show that you understand the other person and what's important to them.

Communicating

We can express ourselves with great clarity and still fail to communicate.

A speaker conveys the message from the perspective of what's important to him/her.

A listener receives the message from the perspective of what's important to him/her.

Unless *both* the speaker and the listener share the same meaning in the message then the words may be totally lost and meaningless.

The key

The key, whether you are a speaker or a listener, is to *show that you understand*. This will give a very clear indication that you are aware of and respectful of the other person's needs, interests, fears and concerns.

If you can do this then the person that you are communicating with will begin to have trust in you. They will want to share information with you and join with you in either a conversation or a relationship. If you cannot demonstrate understanding then the end result may be that the other person will resist your efforts at communication and seek to undermine and avoid conversation and a deeper relationship with you.

Empathy

Every conflict has two components – an **emotional component** and a **rational component.**

Empathy is the ability to imagine yourself in someone else's position and to understand or intuit what that person is *feeling* – to be able to sense their pain or discomfort and respond to it.

The *key thing* to remember – **acknowledge a person's emotional state with an empathic response.**

The rules for good listeners

1. Listen for understanding

    – what important message is the speaker trying to convey?

2. Empathise with the speaker

    – discern and respond to the mood of the speaker.

3. Reflect/playback what you heard

    – summarise or paraphrase.

4. Feedback your interpretation

    – say what you feel and think in response to the speaker's message.

We need to:

- Show that we understood what the person said

- Recognise how they feel about it

- Give some feedback regarding how we feel about the message.

Good listening and conversation is at the heart of every successful relationship and poor listening and conversation is the root of many relationship breakdowns and the basis of most conflicts and disputes.

True listening is a very courageous act because it involves seriously entertaining the ideas, values and perceptions of the other person and putting your own ideas and instinctive responses on hold while you do so.

> *"We cannot find personal intimacy without listening. When we are listening, we are offering the other person the gift of understanding and acceptance (not agreement) – the gift of taking that person seriously."*
>
> — Anon

10: Get your priorities right

Seeing the 'big picture' and focusing on what matters most is a great way to get issues in perspective when you begin the search for solutions.

Finding the time and the space to take a step back from our problems and to see the big picture can be an important step on the way to resolution.

There are three important steps that we can take:

1. Share the story

2. Separate the people from the problem

3. Focus on the future and not the past.

Share your story

Find someone who will *listen* to your story without judging or critiquing.

Alternatively, you could record yourself telling the story.

Listen to yourself as you tell the story.

Challenge any assumptions you may be making about the person with whom you are having the problem. Ask 'What if?' your assumptions were not correct.

Trying to understand what may be driving the other person's view is also an important part of storytelling.

Separate the people from the problem

Try to separate the **who** from the **what** in your situation.

Deal with the people issues separately from the substantive issues.

The difference is often in people's thinking about the problem rather than in the problem itself.

Find ways to manage understand and acknowledge what others are thinking and feeling. See that they are vulnerable human beings too.

Then you can sit side-by-side as problem-solving partners rather than adversaries and face the common task of trying to find a solution to the problem.

Focus on the future not the past

A new and different perspective can be gained by focusing on the future and a time when the conflict or dispute no longer exists.

Imagine a point somewhere between one and five years ahead – and describe in detail the circumstances, relationships, feelings etc. In other words, exactly what life might be like when the conflict or dispute is no longer part of the picture.

It can also be helpful to focus on *best outcomes* and *worst outcomes* and to work out exactly what is important in those scenarios.

The best outcome I can expect if agreement is not reached	
The worst outcome I can expect if agreement is not reached	

11: Find a third party to help

There are huge benefits to bringing in a third party to help you resolve your dispute.

What to look for

Look for a trained or professional mediator to act as a trusted third party.

The best mediators have a natural ability to gain trust and rapport, they understand the dynamics of dispute, how and why warring parties behave as they do, how to listen and how to ask effective questions to uncover hidden interests and agendas. They are also skilled in managing strong emotions and diverse personalities and perspectives.

The *expertly skilled* mediator will help the people involved to form a deeper understanding of the dispute and of the underlying motives and behaviours of all concerned.

Sometimes acting as a confident to each party separately, he or she can help them to transform their attitude towards the dispute, to reach a deep level of honesty and empathy and to explore different options as to how it might be resolved and in the end transcended.

The magic of mediation occurs when those involved finally come to see the vulnerable human beings behind the demons masks they had perceived and are able to move beyond the dispute itself by listening, learning and discovering about themselves as well as each other.

Don't leave it too late

The best time for a mediator to become involved is when direct, face-to-face communication between those involved is no longer possible, where mistrust and suspicion are manifest and where damage and costs, both human and financial, are beginning to escalate.

12: Have a plan in place

Having an agreed system or plan for handling conflicts can help us to manage them more easily and at a much earlier stage and so avoid the problems and costs of escalation.

Know when to act

If we allow a conflict to grow and to fester for too long it will be much harder to manage and more likely to cause *damage and loss*. If, on the other hand, we can find ways for it to be brought to the surface, acknowledged and dealt with then we create the potential to *add value* by finding solutions and repairing relationships.

When people are faced with conflict and they don't know what to do next they often spend too much money, time and emotional energy trying to resolve their problems.

Design a system

A basic design for a Conflict Management System might look as follows:

Level 1: Direct negotiation – the people involved are usually in the best position to attempt to resolve an issue provided that they have:

- Acknowledged the problem

- Not started the adversarial 'blame game'

- The skills and

- Are prepared to devote the necessary time to do so.

Level 2: Assisted negotiation – involving an independent third party who is not, in any way, involved in the issues between the parties is often the next best step. In an organisational setting this might be a trained mediator or facilitator, but in a family setting may be a trusted friend, acquaintance or family member.

Level 3: Formal resolution – if steps 1 and 2 fail to provide a satisfactory resolution then the issue may (if appropriate) be referred to a higher authority – a tribunal or a court or to a more senior person who can make a decision for those involved.

Agree the details that are needed to make it work such as:

- WHO instigates each step

- HOW do they do it

- By WHEN do things have to happen

- WHO needs to be involved

- WHEN is it OK to move on to the next step.

Involve stakeholders

Ideally, all the people who might use the system should be involved in some way or have some say in its design.

The chosen design should present a *preferred path* to resolution starting at the simplest level with the parties themselves and giving clear guidelines about when and how to escalate the matter to the next level.

if issues are flagged up at an early stage when there is still an opportunity to save and even rescue relationships, then the work of planning ahead and designing a system, however simple, may be worth the time and effort.

13: Celebrate differences

In the end, conflicts are resolved by those people who can acknowledge the humanity and celebrate the differences of their opponents.

Differences are normal

Conflict is everywhere – at home and at work, and in society at large between business, partners, spouses, parents and children, religions and countries. At its simplest it is an expression of unmet expectations, when what we get does not match what we *thought* we would get.

Without difference we would live in a zero-sum world without any possibility to add value or grow.

Change your attitude

We cannot ignore conflict in the hope that it will go away or assume that we can fight to defend our position.

The better option is to change our attitude to conflict.

Accept the gift

Conflict is a gift precisely because it highlights the differences between us. If we can dare to be different then we can begin to look for the value rather than for the threat in that difference.

To accept the gift of conflict, we must dare to be different and to look beyond our differences to understand each human being as a unique individual and to embrace the possibilities presented to us.

We must be:

- Willing to seek to understand each other

- Ready to change ourselves

- Prepared to collaborate to find value.

14: Become a Peacemaker

We have to begin to conceptualise our world in a different way if we are to survive the 21st century.

Learning and applying the skills of collaboration at home and at work can transform our lives. What is also needed is a new mode of co-existence for the whole planet.

It has been established that the adversarial approach to relationships is a bad business model. The new approach requires:

1. A better business model and

2. For organisations to join together to share knowledge and commitment.

The starting point is a covenant or pledge in which organisations collectively express their commitment to the principles of corporate peacemaking as the true leaders of the new millennium.

> *"Peacemaking is not something that we should do to or impose on others, it is the responsibility of us all to live its message."*
>
> — Jane Gunn

We may be at the beginning of a new movement away from adversity and towards collaboration, but each small step by each individual person will make a significant difference.

> *"If we listen attentively, we shall hear amid the uproar of empires and nations, the faint fluttering of wings, the gentle stirring of life and hope. Some say this hope lies in a nation, others in a man. I believe, rather, that it is awakened, revived, nourished by millions of solitary individuals whose deeds and words every day negate frontiers and the crudest implications of history."*
>
> — Albert Camus

FURTHER READING

Peace is this Way by Deepak Chopra
Rider Random House, 2005

*Designing Conflict Management Systems - A Guide to Creating
Productive and Healthy Organisations* by Cathy A Constantino and
Christina Sickles Merchant
Jossey-Bass, 1996

The Magic of Conflict: Turning a Life of Work into a Work of Art by
Thomas F Crum
Touchstone/Simon & Schuster, 1987

Making Terrorism History by Scilla Elworthy and
Gabrielle Rifkind
Rider/Random House, 2006

Getting to Yes – Negotiating Agreement Without Giving In by Roger
Fisher and William Ury
Hutchison & Co, 1982

Beyond Reason - Using Emotions as You Negotiate by Roger Fisher and
Daniel Shapiro
Random House, 2005

*Getting Ready to Negotiate - The Getting to Yes Workbook. A Step by
Step Guide to Preparing for any Negotiation* by Roger Fisher
and Danny Ertel
Penguin, 1995

Perfect People Skills - All You Need to Get It Right First Time by Andrew
Floyer Acland
Random House, 2003

Why Love Matters – How affection shapes a baby's brain
by Sue Gerhardt
Routledge, 2004

Make Peace with Anyone: breakthrough strategies to quickly end any conflict, feud or estrangement by David J Lieberman
St Martin's Friffin, 2002

The Finger Book by John Manning
Faber and Faber, 2008

Why Men Don't Listen and Women Can't Read Maps by Alan and Barbara Pease
Orion - PTI, 1998

A Whole new mind. How to thrive in the new conceptual age by Daniel H Pink
Cyan books, 2005

The Dignity of Difference - How to avoid the Clash of Civilizations by Jonathan Sacks
Continuum, 2002

The Survivor Personality by Al Siebert
Practical Psychology Press, 1994

How to Argue and Win Every Time by Gerry Spence
Sidgwick and Jackson/Macmillan, 1996

The Third Side - Why We Fight and How We Can Stop by William Ury
Penguin, 2002

Note on references: If I have inadvertently used any words or materials without acknowledging the originator, I apologise and would be happy to include a reference in the next edition.

NOTES

....
....
....
....
....
....
....
....
....
....
....
....
....
....
....
....
....
....
....
....
....

....

....

....

....

....

....

....

....

....

....

....

....

....

....

....

....

....

....

....

"I've learnt that everyone wants to live on top of the mountain, but all the happiness and growth occurs while you're climbing it."

— Anon

NOTES

....

....

....

....

....

....

....

....

....

....

....

....

....

....

....

....

....

....

....

....

> *"Love is saying 'I feel differently' instead of 'you're wrong'."*
>
> – Anon

NOTES

....
....
....
....
....
....
....
....
....
....
....
....
....
....
....
....
....
....
....

> *"The Earth is too small a star and we too*
> *brief a visitor upon it for anything to matter*
> *more than the struggle for peace."*
> — Colman McCarthy

JANE GUNN

MAKING MOLEHILLS OUT OF MOUNTAINS

Jane Gunn is known as as The Corporate Peacemaker and specialises in advising organisations how to REDUCE THE COSTS (human and financial) of conflict and dispute in both their internal operations and external trading relationships and personal relationships.

A former city solicitor, Jane has now built an international reputation as a mediator, conflict management consultant and speaker working with businesses and business leaders around the world.

Jane's skill is in providing valuable insight and wisdom into how to identify and manage unhappiness and conflict at an early stage before it escalates and becomes both damaging and costly. She saves high profile organisations and busy executives both MONEY and HEARTACHE.

Keynote Speaking

Jane is sought after as a speaker on the international speaking circuit.

Conference keynotes, concurrent and breakout sessions are available as well as half and full day programmes.

Participants are engaged and entertained by a mix of

- Memorable stories
- Current research
- Takeaway skills and tools
- Lively humour.

Jane is a member of the Professional Speakers Association and of the International Federation For Professional Speakers.

Consulting

Jane works with individuals, partners, teams and entire organisations to help them to manage ongoing conflicts and prevent them escalating into costly litigation or other adversarial processes.

She also helps organisations to design Conflict Management Systems enabling them to collaborate with internal departments and external trading partners to identify potential conflicts at the earliest possible stage.

Conflict Management helps businesses whether large or small to

- ADD VALUE by identifying opportunities for change
- AVOID LOSS of profits, productivity and valuable relationships.

Mediation

Jane is frequently called upon to act as a neutral third party to facilitate the resolution of disputes between businesses and individuals.

As one of the leading mediators in the UK, she has over 12 years experience, and has mediated a wide variety of disputes including, business, partnership, employment, property and construction, personal injury and clinical negligence, trusts and family disputes.

Accredited by CEDR in 1996 she is a Mediator Fellow of the Chartered Institute of Arbitrators and International Mediation Institute (IMI) Certified Mediator.

What Jane's Clients Say

> *Jane has a natural affinity with her audience and is clearly at the top of her game in the world of Conflict Management. She has constant insight to offer and the organization that secures her services would do well to pay her enormous sums of money!*

> — James Pirrie, Partner FLIP

Jane is an excellent presenter and speaker, presenting in a practical and humorous manner, which teaches every individual in her audience in a comfortable and effortless style. As a result, the wealth of Jane's experience and knowledge is easily imparted to her audience in a very personal and professional manner.

— Stuart Ness, Director, Rosmartin Associates

Jane has a charming and fun personality, but also a natural sensitivity and perception to the commercial and emotional needs of others. She is also very relaxed at handling and managing people irrespective of their roles, status, age or nationality. All of this makes it easy for her to overcome the barriers to communication at all levels and to facilitate problem-solving.

— Karen Jones, Solicitor, Matthew, Arnold and Baldwin

Armed with her excellent skills, Jane has successfully assisted us in reaching resolution of some very difficult cases using her unique ability to be fair and open to both parties involved. I believe that no party involved in these came away from the experience with anything but respect for the process and Jane's excellent mediation skills.

— Stephanie Seigne, Head of Legal Services & Corporate Risk

Jane is a highly ambitious individual, comfortable working under pressure with tight deadlines and eager to pursue her vision of a peaceful world. Through her communication and interpersonal skills, her skills in relationship management, business development and law, and her deep interest in international affairs, Jane always delivers consistently high standards of work.

— Bob Battye, Chairman, Vistage International

To find out more please contact Jane:
Jane.Gunn@corpeace.com

or visit her website **www.corpeace.com**

To receive your FREE Report

"How Conflict Adds Value" email me direct at

jane.gunn@corpeace.com

or go to **www.corpeace.com**